MES~~SENGER~~

M000196819

The MESSENGER

THE JOURNEY OF A SPIRITUAL TEACHER

BY GEOFF BOLTWOOD

WITH

ANTHEA COURTENAY

PIATKUS

First published in 1994 by
Judy Piatkus (Publishers) Ltd
5 Windmill Street, London W1P 1HF

First paperback edition 1995

The moral right of the author has been asserted

A catalogue record for this book is
available from the British Library

ISBN 0 – 7499 – 1372 – X hbk
ISBN 0 – 7499 – 1458 – 0 pbk

Set in Compugraphic Bakerville by
Action Typesetting Limited, Gloucester

Printed in Great Britain by Bookcraft (Bath) Limited

To Karen

I would really like to acknowledge everyone
who has passed through my life.
So if you have, thank you.

Contents

Introduction

My life began when I was five. I was in hospital, seriously ill with nephritis and rheumatic fever. I have since been told that for a moment I died. Then, an event occurred which not only healed me, but gave me the ability to heal others.

At that moment – and it was only a moment – I was filled with what I later came to call 'Source Energy'. It was the real start of my life, and of my psychic and healing abilities. This spiritual energy has remained with me ever since, leading me along an often difficult and puzzling route; I have spent much of my life discovering why I am here. It is as if I have been carrying sealed orders, which I have been allowed to open little by little, at particular points on my journey.

A large part of my life has been given to healing people; in the main they have come to me with illnesses and other physical problems, but healing is only part of my gifts. Giving healing is a powerful way to open people's perceptions to a spiritual message.

It was Source Energy which eventually led me to take part in successful healing experiments with scientists, and which has enabled me to produce unusual phenomena, like the crystals and scented oils that can appear in my hands when I give healing, and the ability to produce sounds from crystals. Recently it has been channelling information through me about the workings of the human mind and spirit, and how they are changing and must continue to change, for the future of humanity and the planet.

It has not been an easy path. Co-existing with an energy as yet unexplained by science is a double-edged privilege for anyone trying to live in the Western world. So while this book is about my spiritual development, I shall also aim to give an honest account of my life and development as a human being.

I have never kept diaries, and my sense of time is fluid, to say the least. So while my memories of events are clear, their dating and order may not always be totally accurate. As far as possible I have checked the timing of events with any other people involved. If the dating is sometimes inaccurate, I apologise. What is important is the intrinsic truth of my story.

1

The
Healing
Light

My memories until the age of five are very sparse. Before my illness I was an ordinary, somewhat inoffensive little boy, living happily with my parents and older sister in the East End of London. My father owned and ran a café for many years in the then thriving dock area which has since become Docklands, and we lived in a rented terraced house in Stepney, now Tower Hamlets. Between them, my parents provided me with a good background for the different attitudes I was to meet with later in life. My mother was very intuitive, even psychic, and she often had premonitions. This meant that there was someone with understanding in the family when my own psychic abilities opened up.

My Dad, by contrast, though a very kind and loving man, was a total disbeliever in anything non-material. He considered that religion was bunk, the paranormal was bunk, that you lived, you died, and that was the end of it. He would express these views quite vehemently, and my mother accepted this, having evidently decided that arguing about it would be pointless.

As far as I remember it was a secure childhood, undisturbed by family or other dramas until that Saturday in 1953 when, aged five, I was suddenly taken ill. I didn't in fact feel ill, but that morning when I went to the toilet I was intrigued to see that what was coming out was blood. I told my parents, and there was instant panic.

I remember the rest of that day like a series of snapshots with no time-shift between: my parents panicking, the doctor suddenly at our house, and next minute arriving at the local children's hospital, the Queen Elizabeth Hospital for Children. Then I was in a room being examined by a strange doctor.

I was left alone for a time. Then my parents were there, telling me: 'We're going to have to leave you here for a few days.' Why were they leaving me? It felt as if I was being kept in as a punishment.

The next scene: a long room full of beds, a brisk nurse telling me to change into a strange pair of pyjamas. By now I was feeling extremely unwell, probably less due to the illness than because I was in a state of absolute terror.

Another time-jump: my parents kissing me goodbye, smiling as they turned to leave. If their smiles were meant to reassure me, they didn't: I was mystified and terrified. Now I understand that my parents weren't allowed to stay any longer. Then, not knowing when or even whether I would see them again, I watched their retreating figures with mounting distress. Only years later did I realise fully how very alone and abandoned I felt, and how important that was to my development.

My parents visited me daily for the one permitted hour. The rest of the time I was in the hands of the medical staff who, while efficient and caring in their terms, scarcely fulfilled my emotional needs. Once I wet the bed, and was made to wear a girl's nightdress as a punishment. No one explained to me the whys and wherefores of what was done to me. I remember two nurses discussing me one day over my head; one remarked, 'We'll have to have his bowels open tomorrow.' I thought they were going to cut me open, and waited in trepidation for the trolley to come and fetch me. I knew operations were pretty awful, because I'd seen other children being injected and taken away, to return pale and sick.

During the first couple of weeks my condition grew steadily worse. My disease had been diagnosed as nephritis; the blood in my urine had been the first sign that my kidneys were failing. I had daily injections of what I now know was penicillin, and was given iron tablets which I chewed because I couldn't bear to swallow them whole. They were disgusting; the nurses pulled faces as they watched me eating them.

Despite the treatment, I became very ill indeed; my temperature began to climb, and it was found that I also had rheumatic fever which I must have caught in hospital. Because rheumatic fever affects the heart and the joints, the treatment involved lying flat, with no pillows, and totally still. I was constantly being told: 'You must not move.' For a five-year-old, this is not easy.

You do not have to be locked up to be in prison. The experience has enabled me to empathise with people whose lives are restricted by circumstances or by pain. At the time, it was a frustrating, painful period which faded into a kind of muzziness as the fever took over. My condition deteriorated badly, and my temperature soared to 104 degrees.

I had been in hospital for five or six weeks, and my illness was at its worst. It seems possible that I could have died. What happened next was a kind of rebirth. Although it all took place in a flash, I remember the whole event with total clarity.

I was lying in bed in my feverish, muzzy state when suddenly, as if someone had turned on a switch, I was looking at a huge light. It was pure, white and blinding, in front of me and all around me, growing brighter and brighter by the second.

Then I heard a Voice, a deep, loud Voice, saying: 'You will get better now.'

After the Voice had spoken, the light seemed to come towards me; it surrounded and enveloped me totally and entered my body in a powerful rush. I felt all tingly and electric and strange inside. Suddenly I was very awake, very clear-headed and full of energy.

I lay there for a moment wondering whether anyone else had noticed. The Voice had been absolutely booming, yet no one seemed to have heard it. Nobody rushed up to my bed, and I said nothing. But the feverish fugginess had gone. I was quite lucid, in a way I hadn't been for weeks. I was aware of the huge hospital ward full of kids; I was aware of the bed, the noises around me, people talking. I could see the other children; the boy in the next bed was saying his prayers – we often used to say them together.

Then, I simply turned over and went to sleep. The next morning, I was better.

The hospital staff were pleased, but treated my recovery with caution. I was allowed up but I had lost a lot of weight; I was too weak to walk, and had to have physiotherapy. But inside I felt good, and all buzzy.

I said nothing to anybody about my experience, not

even to my parents. Somehow, whenever I saw them it just didn't come into my mind, almost as if it was blanked out, or as if something was telling me, 'It's not the right time to say anything.'

I have only recently discovered the full meaning of much that happened in my childhood. It was a long time before I learned that, at that extraordinary moment, what I have come to call Source Energy entered my body and my entire system, enabling me to work with it, and it with me. Many years later, the Voice which was to become part of my life told me that at that time my heart had briefly stopped.

I am not alone among healers who have had a serious illness in childhood. Shamans, the healers or witch-doctors of ancient cultures, traditionally begin life as sickly children who undergo some kind of healing event or initiation. For me, and presumably for others like me, this was not a miraculous 'healing'; rather, my illness provided the opportunity for the Source Energy to implant itself in me. Since then, it has lived within me, resonating with me, becoming more and more who I really am.

While I had no conscious understanding of what had happened to me, the immediate effect of my rebirth was a striking change in my personality. I felt like a different person. Before the illness I had been a thin, delicate, rather shy child. Now I had become totally unafraid of authority. I was also aware of being different from other children, and although at the age of five I could not analyse it, I knew that this was somehow connected with the Light and the Voice.

My recovery did not end my troubles. Although I felt quite well the doctors said I needed building up, and I had to stay in hospital for several more weeks. There my new defiant personality began making itself felt. I became notorious for my guerilla tactics – for instance with the hospital spinach. Rather than eat this hideous, unappetising paste, I used to stuff it under my pillow, so the nurses had to change all my bed linen. I repeated this operation until they abandoned their efforts at making me eat it. In the long run, this rebellious streak has stood me in good stead: it helped me to develop the ability to stand by what I do. At the time, I must have been insufferable.

As I grew stronger, the doctors decided I needed to convalesce at a children's nursing home at Broadstairs in Kent. Once again, I was informed in the briefest way: 'You are going away for a while to help you feel better.'

Still a very pleasant, unspoilt seaside resort, Broadstairs has the most awful memories for me. My parents and a hospital nurse took me there by train and left me in the home where I was to stay for six or seven weeks with other convalescent children. Once again, I felt deserted.

We were taken regularly to the beach, but in the institutional atmosphere I felt imprisoned, and I was no longer comfortable with other children. Before my illness I had had my normal share of childhood friends. At Broadstairs I didn't like the other children, and didn't want to mix with them. Food was still a contentious issue. Every morning we had to drink hot milk out of tin mugs, and every day we were given bread and honey. To this day the very thought of hot milk makes me feel sick, and I can't go near honey.

The nurses took an instant dislike to this unco-operative little boy, and when they spotted an opportunity to get me, I was got! They probably saw their behaviour as good disciplinary treatment, but some of it was unkind. Once I came down to breakfast with a button done up wrong and a nurse shouted: 'What's the matter with you? You can't even dress yourself properly!' I was only six.

When I had put on enough weight and was able to run around again, I was considered cured and allowed to go home. I still had to visit the hospital for a while because a faulty valve had been found in my heart, a common effect of rheumatic fever. It cleared up in due course without treatment.

When I finally came home, after more than five months away, I was made a great fuss of. Everyone in Belgrave Street came out to welcome me, and I loved all the attention. In those days – not all that long ago – there was quite a village-like atmosphere in those terraced East End streets. We all knew each other and there was a lot of trust; people had keys to each others' houses, or simply left their doors unlocked, so that we children could walk into each other's homes. We could safely play ball games in the street, and child molesters were unheard of.

My mother immediately started spoiling me rotten. After the first flush of homecoming my Dad, probably rightly, pointed out that I was being spoilt and tried not to make things too special for me. Mum took no notice; she waited on me hand and foot, and anything I wanted was instantly produced. Shirley, my sister, was twelve years older than me and now eighteen; I think she regarded me as a bit of a blot.

But for my mother, nothing was too much trouble. I had been ill; I could have died (no one knew that for a moment I actually had). She treated me like a small pasha, and in many ways this was lovely. For several years I never touched the washing up or tidied my room; I was waited on and given treats, and didn't go to bed until I wanted to. The disadvantage was that all the maternal love which enveloped me became a protective cocoon which may have led to a fear of change. Yet my life has consisted of constant change.

Three or four weeks after the general excitement of my return had settled down, I started back at primary school. It was a small, friendly Church of England school, chosen not for its religious affiliations but because it was near our home and had a good reputation educationally.

I was now six. After missing five months' schooling I found it quite hard to catch up. In addition my sense of being different from the others continued, even among my former friends, and a feeling of puzzlement set in. In fact I spent most of my childhood not unhappily, but in a state of great perplexity. This was emphasized soon after my return to school, when odd things started happening at home. They began with the lights switching themselves on and off.

By local standards we were quite well off and were the first family in the street to have a television set – it filled up half the room. We would gather together to watch in the dark, as everyone did then, with the lights off and the blinds down. At bedtime my parents would turn off the set and put on the light. And then the light would turn itself off again.

Dad worked long hours; he got up at four-thirty to serve breakfast at his café, followed by lunch and an evening meal. When he went to bed around ten, he would put the lights out. The next morning, they would be on again. I never liked our living room; I found it creepy especially in the dark, which may be why the lights came on in there more often than anywhere else. But they would also come on during the night in the bedroom I shared with my sister.

Though I didn't know how or why, I knew that it was something to do with me because I could feel something prickly in my body when it happened, which was always just after I had gone into or out of the room. But I said nothing. My mother certainly recognised what was happening as a psychic phenomenon and calmly accepted it, though she may not have connected it with me. My Dad invariably put it down to a fault in a switch.

The lights going on and off were the first of several odd physical effects of my influx of energy. Looking back, they were like an announcement that something was beginning, a symbolic message: 'Something's coming, it's going to grow. The light's coming, and you are going to see.'

There followed a whole range of poltergeist activities including inexplicable noises and knockings, which went on for about a year. We could all hear the bangs and raps; my Dad put them down to the age of the house. The phenomena really took off when we heard notes coming from the piano when no one was in the living room. This happened a lot, and we all heard it.

Dad's response to the piano playing itself was my first experience of the 'logical explanation' which is completely illogical. The living room door was shut, the piano lid was closed, and our cat was out of the house. But Dad explained – always after the event – that the notes were obviously caused by the cat walking over the piano keys. He never actually went in at the time to look.

I did not get on badly with my father, but it was inevitable that I should feel closer to my mother. I accepted Dad as he was; indeed I cared about him and would have been very upset if anything had happened to him. But we were not emotionally close. It wasn't until the last year of his life, when I was in my twenties, that I developed a closer link with him. His illness drew us together, and at this time I realised that within this vehemently sceptical man was someone who was quite afraid.

While these curious events were going on at home, my new rebellious character was making itself felt at school. To my schoolmates and teachers I must have seemed an arrogant little sod. In fact, for a while I was very psychologically withdrawn. Doubtless a psychologist would put my personality change down to my separation from my parents; after all, I had been taken to hospital one Saturday morning and dumped there, virtually without explanation. But the presence of the energy inside me, which I did not yet understand, was nevertheless very powerful; I knew I was somehow not like other people.

Part of me was quite detached and unchildlike. I didn't really enjoy or want the company of people my own age. I found their behaviour difficult to understand. What did they get out of running round the playground shouting? I wasn't unfriendly but at playtime, though I joined in because it was expected of me, I would rather have sat and read a book. I had an almost arrogant feeling that all these people around me were wasting their time doing silly things. They didn't seem to understand, or know, or feel, or see any of the things that I was interested in.

It was not only that I felt different from my schoolmates; I also found adult behaviour hard to understand. Later, for instance, one of the punishments we were given at school was to copy out poems. To me, this was a pleasurable activity – why was it a punishment? When they wanted me to do something that to me seemed unjustified, it was natural to me to argue about it; inside, I felt I was their equal, and I genuinely couldn't see in them the authority they were trying to exert over me. But they had no idea of considering my point of view and dismissed my behaviour as sheer damned awkwardness.

At that time schoolchildren were given daily milk and cod liver oil capsules. Before my illness I drank my milk and took my capsule, because the teachers told me to. When I went back, I said, 'I don't want them.'

They tried everything from 'It's good for you' to 'You must!' They shouted at me; they reasoned with me. I simply wouldn't drink the milk and I wouldn't take the cod liver oil capsule.

This battle went on for days: it was the teachers who gave up. As far as I remember I was the only boy in the class who didn't down his milk. From my point of view, what must have appeared as rebellion to the teachers was simply a strong inner feeling of: 'I'm not a little child any more. I know more than you do. You can't do this to me!'

I behaved during lessons, but whenever I thought I was being treated unjustly I would say so. Before I went to hospital, I had found the teachers quite awesome; we all did as we were told. Now, I had completely lost my fear of them. Particularly ferocious was Mr Brock, who taught the older children; he was known as a powerful person, who used the cane. My first confrontation with him was at school dinner, which he supervised. I didn't like fat on meat; at home I was allowed to cut it off, so I cut the fat off my school meat.

'Eat your fat,' said Mr Brock.

'No,' I said. 'I don't eat fat.'

'You won't leave the table until you do.'

I said, 'All right. I won't leave the table.' I was quite content to sit there all day. Mr Brock bellowed and screamed at me, but nothing in me quaked. He lost. I didn't eat my fat.

I told my Mum I wasn't having school dinners any more, and why. She said, 'OK, you come home for dinner then.' I was lucky in having a mother who was at home full-time in those days. Later, things got difficult for my father and she had to go out to work. But there was always someone there for me: our landlady, who lived in the basement, was like one of the family, and I called her Nanny. When my mother was out she cooked for me, and spoiled me rotten too.

Another discovery, during the phase of poltergeist phenomena at home, was that I could make small objects move by pointing at them without touching them. This intrigued me, and when I was on my own in the bedroom I used to practise making things move.

Although I wasn't very sociable, I had one good school friend, Tony. One reason I liked him was that we enjoyed using our imaginations together in play; we would go on imaginary journeys, and talk about magic spells. Tony didn't know about the odd things that were happening to me, but one day I had an impulse to share my secret with him. We had some of the wax crayons given out in art classes, and I told him: 'I can make these crayons move.' He looked disbelieving, so I decided to show him. I put my hand out and succeeded in getting two or three crayons to jump.

Suddenly all the fun and all the imagination just went. Tony was never as friendly again. It was OK to imagine things in play; real magic was too much for him.

I had learnt a lesson about not being too open. After this, perhaps protected by inner or higher guidance, I chose to tell no one about my gifts. Again, I felt my difference from other people. I knew there was a reason for it, and I knew it was something to do with what had happened in hospital, though just what I did not understand.

Quite soon after this, I started seeing people invisible to others. One day we were visiting my grandmother, who shared a house with another old lady. They were chatting with my mother and I was wondering when we were going home, when I saw between them another lady who had no colour. She was elderly, dressed in contemporary clothes and quite solid, but everything about her was white: her hair, skin and clothes were all white. I wasn't at all frightened, though it was fairly obvious that nobody else could see her. But I was still fairly withdrawn; I felt apprehensive about speaking about it, and said nothing.

Soon after this I came home from school one afternoon and went down to the basement where our landlady lived. She wasn't there, but there was a friendly man in overalls, wielding a bucket of paint and brushes. He told me his name was Fred and he was doing some work in the house. He asked me how I was getting on at school, and we had quite a long, perfectly normal, adult – child conversation.

Then I went upstairs for my tea. Four slices of bread and butter, without honey, always awaited me after school, and a cup of tea, to keep me going for the hour and a half before our evening meal; I was still being spoilt, and I had a huge appetite.

Over tea, I told Mum that I had met Fred downstairs. She looked puzzled and said, 'But there's nobody there.' We went downstairs together, and indeed no one was there.

My mother sat me down and said, 'Tell me what happened.'

I told her what I had seen. Mum said, 'Nanny's brother Fred used to live here years ago, he did decorating for a living. He died twenty years before you were born.' She added, 'It's nothing to worry about; he just came back to say hallo. When people die, it's just their body that dies, and they go on living as spirits. And sometimes their spirits come back for a visit. There's nothing to be afraid of.'

In fact I hadn't been at all frightened; there had been nothing to be frightened of. But then I told my mother that I had seen other people, and she asked me to let her know when I saw any more. After that I told her whenever I saw people no one else could see; they were nearly always people she could recognise from my descriptions.

My mother herself had the rather unfortunate faculty of being able to see when someone was going to fall ill and die. For example, she once saw a friend's husband pass quickly by without acknowledging her; later she learned that he had been somewhere else at the time. At that time no one knew that he was ill, but a few months later he died. This kind of incident happened quite frequently. The figure she glimpsed was what many psychics call the astral body, apparently preparing to leave the physical.

I began seeing constantly what my mother called 'spirit' people. Whenever we went visiting they would be standing among the people we had gone to see. The interesting thing is that while Fred had looked normal and in full colour, the people I saw were often very white, like the woman at my grandmother's. They never spoke, though they might smile. Apart from their lack of colour they looked quite ordinary and solid – though they would sometimes simply disappear. I got used to them suddenly vanishing; it didn't alarm me.

When my mother talked to my father about all this he put it down to childish imagination, which I would duly 'grow out of'. As far as he was concerned, life was a strange quirk, and at the end you went back to being a collection of chemicals; he couldn't relate to spirits or ghosts. Throughout my childhood, if ever the subject came up he would become very irritable, and I quickly got the message not to discuss it with him. Very much later, he told me how during his Air Force days in the war he had accompanied a group of young men to a graveyard to 'raise the spirits'; they all saw 'something' and ran away. This may indicate that he was psychic himself, but very afraid of it.

I saw figures in our own house, too, and often when I was in the garden I would glance up and see people standing looking out of the windows. They would just appear at the window looking out, and then disappear.

There was a stage during which these sightings came quite intensively. After a while it became apparent that these people and I could communicate; we certainly exchanged smiles. Perhaps we could have communicated telepathically, but I didn't consider this possibility. The totally real conversation with Fred was a remarkable and very unusual experience, though I didn't know that at the time.

There was only one occasion when I was frightened – it was the first and last time. I went into the living room and saw a very tall, dark man standing there; there was something sinister-looking about him. When he started laughing out loud, I was really alarmed and ran out into the garden.

My Mum didn't know who he was, but she said, 'This is a very old house and an awful lot of people have lived here. Sometimes people aren't very pleasant, and maybe this man isn't very happy. But he can't hurt you, and he isn't going to hurt you. You won't come to any harm.'

I had other unusual experiences. Never a very good sleeper, I was lying awake one night staring at the bedroom ceiling. Suddenly the ceiling began to move, as if it were liquid. Gradually it broke up into patterns, which turned into a lot of sparkly energy dancing around in all kinds of colours and shapes. I watched, fascinated, as the energy patterns faded away, together with the ceiling, and I found myself looking directly at the sky. The sky too began to change and melt, and in its turn became a complex of energy patterns dancing. Then everything returned to normal. I had enjoyed the display and was fascinated by it, but I didn't think it odd; something inside me knew that it wasn't.

I was in fact being taught. I now know that I was going through the early stages of what was to be a journey of discovery. I have been told through channelling that the Source Energy implanted in me that day in hospital was beginning to come through, preparing me for the future. It was building ideas in me at an early age so that it could gradually educate me towards acquiring the perspective from which I can now work. What has been made clear to me as an adult is that, no matter how powerful that energy, the perception of the mind it is working with has to be changed so that it can use the energy appropriately.

There are a number of people like myself, mainly healers and spiritual teachers, who are not born with special gifts, but in whom Source Energy has been implanted later in life. A few are well known; most of them are not. The Energy has also been implanted at certain critical times in history, in a number of people in different locations.

Only very much later did I fully understand the nature of the Source itself. It is a state of pure potential, which gives rise to all that comes into being, including the stream of Infinite Mind in which our own universe and others are found. Infinite Mind is not controlled by the Source – it is watched over by it, but without interference.

When I speak about the Source many of my listeners assume that it is synonymous with God, but super-imposed on the concept of God are many different, man-made images and beliefs which do not apply to the Source. The Source is not a person, not a spirit, and not an omnipotent being with power over our souls; it is an infinite potential for intelligence, creative power and infinite love, but the ability and free will to draw on and empower that potential lie within ourselves.

At this point in my life, the Source was gently educating me: I was being given by direct experience the knowledge that nothing, including ceilings, is actually solid: that all matter is composed of particles, and operates through a pattern of energy, some of which forms 'solid' things. I have come to realise in addition that there are infinite, intricate patterns of energy mixing these particles together, and that human beings may see only part of the pattern. There are many other patterns which we cannot see, just as we cannot see ultra-violet or X-rays.

All this ties up with recent channelled information I have been given that the physical universe does not exist separately from consciousness. If we all share a physical dimension and see the physical environment in the same way, this is because at one level we all share an integrated Mind.

It became habitual for me to lie in bed and wait for the ceiling to disappear; it happened quite often, and I thought it was wonderful! As time went on I learned that I could make it happen at will: I would lie in bed and say, 'OK, I want the ceiling to melt' – and it would.

The Source was not only showing me things which

later on would make more sense, but by discovering that I could 'make' the ceiling melt I learned that consciousness is an integral part of what's out there. While I did not understand any of this at the age of six, the phenomenon was a practical demonstration which allowed me to see and absorb facts which would help me later to understand the nature of matter.

Experiences like this allowed me to develop a freedom of perception so that in my later work, which is about changing perception, I have a complete and absolute inner knowing that there are doorways between different dimensions or universes, and that by opening them you can change perceived reality. Today, I produce physical phenomena that other people see and hear. To make these things happen for other people, I have to believe that their perception too can be changed.

The ceiling melting was of course my own perception, since I was alone, and to me it was perfectly real. I cannot speak for what others might have perceived had anyone else been present, but I know now that changes of perception can be shared. Meanwhile, discovering that I could make the ceiling melt deepened my sense of being different from others. I shared it with no one, and it only happened when I was alone. But I was beginning to get the feeling that I was special.

Another very odd event happened one night. This too was perfectly lucid; I was not asleep or dreaming. I was lying awake in bed when suddenly the bed seemed to go through the wall, with me in it.

I found myself in a bedroom; a woman and a man whom I didn't know came in; they looked down at me and talked to me as if they knew me. I couldn't speak; I just lay looking up at them. They looked quite real and ordinary, and they seemed to be tucking me in. I tried to say, 'But I don't belong here!' – but nothing would come out of my mouth. Although it seemed quite a while, it was probably only a minute or two before the bed slid through the wall again, and I was back in my bedroom alone.

I believe now that I was being shown how consciousness can travel across time and space. I had moved into a dimension of my own being in which I temporarily slipped into the mind of a child in another dimension, in a universe parallel or alternative to this one. The universe we see around us is simply one of many possible dimensions or alternative universes which exist in parallel with this one, and which some people can enter.

I must have been getting on for seven when my Voice entered the schoolroom. I hadn't heard it since that day in hospital and had never mentioned it to anyone, but I hadn't forgotten it.

We were having religious instruction from Father Marshbank. Youngish, perhaps in his thirties, with a big mop of black hair, he came to teach us dressed in full, flowing clerical garb. Up till then our religious instruction had consisted of various clergymen telling us Bible stories like Daniel in the Lion's Den. Father Marshbank, however, started speaking very fervently about death − a strange thing to launch on a bunch of seven-year-olds. He told us that originally people used to go straight to heaven, and there was no death. But because man had sinned, people had to die, which was why God had sent Jesus to save sinners from death.

It was at this point that my Voice said, very loudly in my ear: 'Don't listen to him.' I knew the Voice could be trusted, and that I could trust absolutely what it said. So I stopped listening to Father Marshbank, and I never listened to religious dogma again.

From then on, every Thursday when we were paraded off to church, I used to sit there and daydream. I never heard a word of the sermon or the lessons. I joined in the hymns because I liked music, but not one bit of religious teaching went in. When I left my excellent church school I had not an ounce of Christian belief in me.

I knew there was a higher power, because I had a direct link with it. But this had nothing to do with the judgmental, demanding 'God' that Father Marshbank and others preached at me. On approaching the age for confirmation, I went to catechism class for one week and then announced firmly, 'I'm not going.' That was it.

From then on, my Voice has spoken to me, guided me and given me loving support. These days it often speaks internally, but when it has something especially important to say I hear it as a clear, external voice, just as I did when I was a child. At that time I didn't question who or what it was. I knew that I had something that no one else seemed to have, and I felt instinctively that I owed it my life.

I also had an inner certainty, even at that early age, that I was here for a purpose, that my 'differentness' was going to lead to something important. For this reason, I never bothered to work very hard at school. My reports always bore the comments: 'Very intelligent, but lazy. Should try harder.' I enjoyed my lessons and did the minimum required, but I knew that schoolwork had no bearing on what I was going to do with my life. In my childhood I was becoming strongly aware of a sense of destiny, though what that destiny was I had no idea.

2

Learning to Be Human

My world changed again when at the age of eleven I left my small, friendly primary school for Dempsey Secondary School. At the same time, my psychic abilities and my contact with my Voice went underground for several years.

It was a difficult time for me. Dempsey, which no longer exists, was a very tough East London school. The teachers were a similar mix to those I had known before; some were disciplinarians, others quite easy-going. But among the boys there was a hierarchy, and of course I arrived on the bottom rung. During the first two or three weeks in the playground the second-year boys would thump all the new boys on the head or the back of the neck at regular intervals. Those who resisted were dragged into the toilets to have water flushed over their heads. I did resist: I simply wouldn't stand it. Perhaps because of the energy within me, although I was not large or physically strong I was somehow able to convey to potential tormentors that if they did anything to me

23

they would be in trouble. I got away with it, too; I was very rarely set upon.

Once again, however, I was an outsider, in more ways than one. At Dempsey it wasn't done to like music or poetry or any of the things that I liked; they were all considered 'cissy'. You were supposed to enjoy football, cricket, engineering and technical drawing, all of which I hated. However, I was never afraid to express my preferences, and when I told my teachers I would rather do English than engineering, for instance, I was allowed to change classes.

I loved English lessons, especially poetry, I even enjoyed Shakespeare; I didn't understand his plays, but I loved the feel of the language. This was something no one was supposed to admit to; the other boys jeered aloud at literature. Perhaps the most important thing I learned at this school was the ability to accept other people's points of view, while sticking to my own. I kept quiet and enjoyed the classes as best I could. I liked science, too, while at home I pursued my innate love of music. I had no formal lessons but could play the piano quite well, if not brilliantly, by ear; I still enjoy playing by ear.

Man-made authority was still meaningless to me. I had terrible battles with some of the staff which, I have to say with some pleasure, I always won – though I now feel sorry for the teachers concerned. I had such an obstinate streak, such a certain knowledge that I wasn't going to do what I didn't want to do, that they hadn't a chance.

The disappearance of my Voice, almost simultaneously with my first day at school, was a great loss. Until then, even when my Voice was silent I had always had a powerful inner feeling that I was not alone. When it left me, I lost that sense of support.

The diminishing of extra-dimensional awareness in

early adolescence is common among psychic children. It seems to be a natural stage of development, enabling them to experience ordinary, everyday life. But it is accompanied by a feeling of barrenness. As anyone on a spiritual path will know, periods of aloneness seem to be a necessary part of the process, whether by literally going into the wilderness or by enduring emotional and spiritual solitude. Secondary school was my wilderness, and I didn't like it one little bit. Not understanding what had happened, I felt quite depressed and sad, and very lonely.

On the other hand, lacking that added dimension forced me to relate to other people and the outside world. I think it was necessary for me to experience both kinds of life, with and without inner support, just as it was important that I had been born to parents with such diverse beliefs. I learned very early on how to contend with feeling different while having to behave like other people. I didn't like feeling ordinary – it was diabolically horrible, in fact; but I had to go through it. And, although my obstinacy never left me, my feelings of arrogance and superiority were considerably tempered during this spiritually empty phase. In some ways I even enjoyed that period, because I felt more integrated than before.

I made a few friends. It was difficult to find people similar to myself, but I learned that you don't have to be the same as someone else to be close to them. I managed to find companions who shared my main interests, music and nature. I had acquired my total love of nature with the early energy, and it never left me. I was at my happiest exploring natural surroundings or looking after animals. Nature of course can be aggressive and bloody, but always in the interests of territory and population control, not driven by the egotistic need for violence for its own sake.

I had one particular friend, Derek – perhaps my only real friend – who accompanied me on insect and caterpillar hunts on the many bomb-damaged sites left over from the war. Not yet rebuilt, and free of chemical sprays, they were miniature nature reserves full of butterflies and wild flowers. We were able to find and collect loads of little creatures. It was a very gentle activity.

My respect for nature was not shared by all my companions. When I was around twelve, I was playing with a group on a piece of wasteland; a spider ran along the wall, and one of the gang suddenly slipped out a box of matches and set light to it. I could actually feel the spider's death; it hurt me. I walked away, appalled.

I loved all creatures, spiders included; I was always rescuing baby birds which probably didn't need rescuing and, to my mother's horror, I collected a menagerie of snakes, lizards and other reptiles which I found odd and interesting. I also used to keep caterpillars and watch them develop into butterflies.

I have always had a deep affinity with butterflies. Throughout my life whenever I've been down, when I've reached the point of wondering what on earth was going to happen next, I've always seen a butterfly. Once, as an adult, I was on the underground in the middle of winter, deep in thought about where my life was going, when a butterfly flew past me. I thought, 'This is nice, it's a message for me, but it must be a hallucination.' It wasn't; it became clear from people's remarks that everyone else could see it too. A butterfly in the middle of winter on the underground is not a usual sight.

A while ago, when I was preparing leaflets for some

workshops, my Voice told me: 'Call your work *Meta-morphosis, Changing Perception*. That is why you have always loved butterflies: they represent the changing of perception from a creature that can't fly to a very different one that can.'

Butterflies have to go through the chrysalis stage before they can spread their wings. Most people following a spiritual path will recognise this stage; it's very unpleasant because you can't move, even though you know you're ultimately going to get out. But it was a long time before I made the very logical link between my fascination with butterflies and the progress of my own life. On a wider scale, I feel that butterflies are particularly relevant to humanity as a whole, which is at the point of emerging into a new, freer stage of evolution.

The development of the butterfly is also a good image of how it feels to have Source Energy inside me. Recently my Voice told me that, even though I have come out of my chrysalis by electing to do the work I now do, I have had to remove my wings and bury them. While I can fly to other dimensions in my mind, being wingless on this planet feels uncomfortable. It's really awkward not being able to fly when and where you want to! There is an occasional sense of longing, a feeling that the energy that is in me has so much potential for expansion, so many dimensions to experience, that being physically here is at times cumbersome. But if I am to relate to other people in the physical world, I have to be in here with them.

Before my psychic awareness died down, I had already acquired the certain knowledge that I had something important to do and that I would do it. So while the loss of my Voice saddened and disturbed me, I knew somehow that it would return. Meanwhile, my intuition was still quite strong. Like my mother, I could feel when people weren't well; I would see a dark cloud around them which told me that someone was about to fall ill. I had a vague feeling of wanting to do something about it, but never had the courage to approach them.

My views on religion had not changed. When I was around thirteen a seven-year-old local child was drowned. The comments of the adults around inspired me to compose a song about his death; it suddenly came back to me while writing this chapter. It is not great literature, but expresses my thoughts at a time when much of our religious teaching simply didn't make sense.

> When Jimmy died he went to heaven,
> That's what my Mummy said.
> Poor little Jimmy was only seven,
> And everybody cried.
> Why did they cry for him?
> For heaven is a place where the angels wait,
> My teacher told me so.
> There's no pain, and no one cries,
> And you live up there for ever more.
> So why did they cry for Jimmy?
>
> When Mr Jones died he went to hell,
> That's what my Mummy said.
> He was a dirty old man, and a drunk as well,
> And not one person cried for him.
> Why didn't they cry for him?
> For hell is a place where the Devil waits,
> My teacher told me so,
> Where fire burns forever more
> Your damned and tormented soul.
> So why did they cry for Jimmy?

As I grew into adolescence, other interests began to pre-occupy me. Like my schoolmates, I went to the pictures, succeeding occasionally in sneaking into X-certificate films. I remember a wonderful moment at school when someone said, 'There's this film on with Brigitte Bardot with no clothes on!' A group of us sneaked into the cinema and sat through the whole film for a one-second vision of loveliness at the end.

Much more fun was the private cinema in my head. At home, I began to spend a good deal of time playing imaginary games. This was the sort of play that children of five and six enjoy, and it's not expected at fourteen or fifteen; but I already had an amazing ability to imagine any reality and spent hours and hours in my bedroom happily imagining.

I would only have to start making up a story and it would unfold as if it were actually happening. It was great fun. I decided I wanted a spacecraft, and there it was, ready-made. I can remember its interior quite clearly: it was big and comfortable with a special screen for instant non-radio communication with other spacecraft. I spent hours and hours in my bedroom devising a whole series of intricate space adventures.

The physical sensation of space-travelling was a delightful weightlessness, as if my body had no density, accompanied by a rush of elation. It was a very joyous experience; I had the ability to move freely and instantly from one spot to another – something like teleportation. I could be outside the house, in the sky among the stars, or in another country, instantaneously. I met people on my travels – ordinary people in the street or in their homes, with whom I was able to communicate mentally.

My imaginary journeys were extraordinarily real; it was rather like a hypnotic state, or like virtual reality. When people say, 'It's only your imagination', there is no 'only' about it. Imagination is a door to other dimensions and realities. What you imagine has a life and reality of its own. It is there. It exists. It is possible that when people see UFOs they are seeing mind-created objects like my own spacecraft, in which someone like myself from another dimension is having fun.

I stayed at Dempsey until I was fifteen. I was potentially quite bright, but never exerted myself academically and to the distress of my parents and teachers I insisted on leaving school with no O-levels. This was a source of conflict, even to me, as I had been brought up to believe that I must learn enough to get a job and earn a living.

At the same time, the idea of going out to work induced in me a shudder of revulsion. A large part of me didn't want to get a job, which would prevent me from exploring my vivid imaginary world. I didn't want to be bored stiff just to earn money. At that time, I didn't want to have to relate to people; my years at Dempsey might have taught me to mix but they hadn't taught me to enjoy being surrounded by people. While my inner development was still going on, I was content with my own company. Now, of course, I am happily surrounded by people for much of the time.

All the same, I badly needed to get out of the school atmosphere and gain some experience of the world. To me, there was no point in staying on. In my mother's eyes I could do no wrong, but my decision led to a few gritted-teeth differences of opinion with my father. I remember telling him that one day I wanted to do some work in other countries, and his comment, 'Without qualifications that'll never happen.' Sadly, he didn't live to see that it could happen, since I now travel abroad regularly.

As usual I got my own way and I left school at the end of the Easter term. It was quite a while before I got a job – not because there were no jobs, but because I obstinately refused to take on anything I didn't want to do. I stayed at home for most of the summer; my parents must have wondered whether I was ever going to start earning a living. It wasn't until the autumn that I got a post as a technician in the Pharmacology Department at Bart's Hospital Medical School, where I stayed for a year.

What my parents didn't know was that during that summer all sorts of fascinating things were happening to me as my psychic gifts returned, with interest. The start of this resurgence coincided with a notable event which must be every young man's dream – my sexual initiation by an attractive, older woman.

That summer the family went to a holiday camp on the Isle of Wight for a couple of weeks. Holiday camps are strange places where lots of strange people are thrown together at social events like dances, games and competitions laid on nightly in the ballroom. One evening I found myself drawn to a young woman called Jacqueline. She was twenty-seven, and very attractive. Totally out of character, I invited her to dance and we spent the rest of the evening together, dancing, watching the games and talking.

When the ballroom closed down we walked by unspoken mutual consent out into the hot, starlit night and down to the beach. There Jacqueline seduced me. The word may sound old-fashioned, but that's what she did. She guided me, told me what to do, where and how to touch, how to take my time. . . . The whole episode was both very strange and totally natural. I must have been clumsy, but she didn't make me feel so. I didn't feel shy or worried. It was a lovely experience. I never saw her again.

One of the nice things about my Voice's ability to stop me absorbing religious teaching was that I had no sense of guilt about sex whatsoever. On the contrary, I had been shown just how natural and right sexual encounters can be. After this thoroughly enjoyable adventure, I had no fear that God was going to strike me down; I just wanted to do it again.

All this brought home to me very early on that sexual energy is totally natural. Many healers, as well as other spiritual and creative people, have a strong sex drive; it is a part of their energy as a whole – one aspect of a positive, creative driving force. Yet society has a kind of expectation that spiritual people must be 'pure', meaning sexless. As a result, the repression of sexuality by 'spiritual' leaders and organisations can lead to genuinely harmful behaviour. It is not unknown for people in positions of emotional or psychological power sexually to exploit their followers or patients. This is a total misuse of both sex and personal power.

Sexual energy is a spiritual energy like any other. In itself it is pure; it is how people use it that colours it. Sexual activity does not always have to be romantic – it can be engaged in purely for fun, so long as it is equally fun for both partners. But it is important to come to terms with your feelings about it, and to treat your partners honestly, thoughtfully and with respect for safety.

It is when sex is accompanied by deception or manipulation that it leads to harm – and deception and manipulation arise out of the very restrictions that society has placed on it. I believe that the guilt and sense of sin attached to sex over the centuries have profoundly distorted human attitudes. Though being free of guilt is not, of course, a licence to behave irresponsibly; responsibility is not the same as guilt.

It seems possible that my unexpected ability to relate to a woman was the first manifestation of my energy re-emerging. Once I was back home, very soon after my initiation on the beach, things started happening for me again. I was still spending a lot of time alone thinking and dreaming, when three major events occurred.

Firstly, I was in my bedroom one evening when my Voice came back. As before, it was an external, quite loud and resonant voice. If asked, I would have said it was male, but I never really considered who or what it was, or tried to imagine its physical appearance.

It said, quite loudly: 'It is time to teach you.'

This would have been all very well if it had said more, but that was it. I was left to mull over this one statement: 'It is time to teach you.'

I have quite often been given these single statements, which are never elaborated on however much I plead. But I always trusted what my Voice said. I thought, 'At last! It's all going to happen.' This feeling was to return over and over again through my life. I have done an awful lot of waiting, and whenever things do start happening, I always feel there is still more to come.

Meanwhile, I suddenly started to write reams of poetry. This was an extremely powerful experience; over a period of two to three weeks I was impelled to sit down to write every evening. The words poured out, absolutely unstoppably, and I filled up four or five exercise books. As poetry it wasn't very good; I still have some of it and wouldn't dream of inflicting it on anybody.

The subject matter was a mixture: some of it was emotional – the normal outpourings of adolescent feelings; some of it was decidedly symbolic. I think it was serving a dual purpose. Part of it was a cleansing process for me. It was like emptying out an emotional dustbin, throwing out of my system a lot of detritus that had gathered over the years.

Other poems seemed to presage ways of connecting with other minds. One or two were about the minds of other poets which entered my own mind when I tried to write. One was Walter de la Mare, and another was Shelley whom I admired very much. In my poems I told them, 'I love you very much for your work, but I want to write something of my own.' But they insisted on helping me, and for a while these poets' minds continued to influence what I wrote.

During this period I had a very profound dream: one of those absolutely lucid dreams which seems completely real. In it, I was taken into a room, and in the room there was a bed with a woman lying on it who was extremely ill. She was covered up, with just her head visible, and she was unconscious. I didn't recognise her. Around the bed stood several people who seemed to know her, all feeling helpless, totally lost, certain she was not going to recover.

I knew with absolute conviction that I could make her better. I was totally above all the suffering and the pain of all these people. I walked up to the bed, took the woman's hand and held it, and she got up. Everybody was overjoyed and they started hugging each other.

At this point, quite abruptly, I woke up.

This dream revived in me the feeling that I had something very, very special, and that it was important. This may sound arrogant, but it is the truth: I did and still do feel special, and that I am here for a reason. I don't mean that I expect or want my name to be on everybody's lips, but I know now that I am here to help the changes in the planetary energy, and that I have to pass my knowledge on.

There followed a short period when the energy burst out again in the form of physical phenomena – lights going on and off, raps on the wall and strange noises in my bedroom. I knew the energy behind them was coming from me, and not from an outside source, and they only happened when I was alone, so I didn't have to contend with my family's comments.

I had a lot of ornaments in my bedroom – little stones I had collected, a family of tin lions and other bits and pieces. I noticed that when I wasn't looking, they would rearrange themselves. To be quite sure I wasn't imagining it I would put them in a certain order every night, and make a note of their positions. For a while I became quite obsessive about it. Overnight, they were definitely rearranged. Sometimes, an object would disappear to reappear a day or so later. I also rediscovered my ability to control the energy by deliberately making them move.

I didn't regard these inanimate objects as dead things. They all had energy. I did something that small children do: if I had a problem to resolve I would choose one of my ornaments, a lion for instance, and talk to it. It helped me to work things out. My vivid imagination made it a very real experience and I would hold quite long conversations. It was not that I believed that the lion was talking, but I used it as a focus to reflect back the answers that were already within me.

My Voice also started communicating with me fairly regularly. On one occasion it referred to my dream, and confirmed that I had been given a gift that I would have to use. It told me that 'they' were working with me, but when I asked who 'they' were I got no reply. It went on to say that I would heal people; this would be the beginning of what I would do, and my work would develop progressively. 'They' had a purpose for me and I must pursue it.

I was told that it was still necessary for me at that time not to share this information; I must keep it to myself, though I would be given the opportunities to use it. The reason for my being here would be made apparent. I mustn't try to go out and start it myself; all I had to do was accept it. The people I needed to meet would be brought to me.

Interestingly enough, at sixteen I found it quite possible to accept all this. I really had no inclination to rush out and say, 'Look folks, I can hear voices and I'm going to heal people!' At this stage I was not given any profound philosophical ideas, but I sometimes received very practical information about people around me – when they were ill, for example. And whereas I had not so far been able to help people who were ill, I now began to project at them the thought of healing, without telling them. Some of them seemed to get better, though I had no way of knowing whether they wouldn't have got better anyway.

With the return of the energy, the feeling also returned of being slightly removed and odd, an outsider. My journeying and Voice communications continued in private. In one way it was good to have the energy back with me, but it also caused me considerable disturbance. There was a phase when it became very intense; I began again to have a shifting of reality: I could see people who weren't there, and was getting spontaneous clairvoyance.

After Bart's, I went to work in the accounts department at Harrods; it was while I was there that the energy was at its most disturbing. I went through a temporary period when my imaginary journeys felt so real that at times I genuinely couldn't distinguish them from real life.

From my point of view, I actually visited places which I could not have done physically, including Egypt and India, which fascinated me. I can remember the foreign smells as I walked along a hot, dusty road, talking with someone. I also loved free-ranging among the stars, and the sense of freedom it gave me. When I travelled in my spacecraft I could see the craft, and handle the controls.

For many psychically gifted people, shifting reality is such a wonderful feeling that it can become like a drug. You have to learn to be in control of your gifts. As with any other talent, total obsession can become destructive both to yourself and to others, particularly if the gifts are not allied to spiritual expansion.

In addition, although experiences like my travels have their own reality, they can sound to other people like a kind of madness, especially when you speak of something as fact which they are convinced *can't* be. This raises the whole question of what madness really is. I think there are a lot of people whose 'insanity' simply consists of seeing things in a different way, which is very difficult for other people to accept.

There were a number of young people working in Harrods' accounts department, and we chatted a good deal during working hours. My conversation often drifted into my second reality, and I would make remarks like, 'I was in Delhi last night talking to a man in the market.' It never occurred to me that what I was saying was impossible; I really forgot that other people might consider the telling of such stories weird. Possibly there was an element, too, of wanting to impress people. I was in fact totally ignoring the instructions of my Voice, which had told me not to speak about these things. Naturally, my office mates began to give me sideways looks.

Fortunately, one of the girls I worked with actually understood the situation. She took me on one side, and said gently, 'There's something wrong – you need to get help. You can't possibly have been to Delhi last night.'

I thought about it and realised what I'd said. I knew I was not mad, but perhaps I did need help of some kind? I went to see the Harrods doctor, who referred me to a psychiatrist. Harrods paid for my visit, which was nice of them.

The psychiatrist was as helpful as he could be, but from my side it was a token visit. I had intended to be open and honest with him, but when I got there I knew that he would not understand my psychic experiences and gave him only half the story. He listened kindly, and decided that I was suffering from a temporary schizophrenic attack, escaping into a fantasy world from an over-stifling home atmosphere. I simply needed to leave home and find a flat on my own, and everything would be fine.

I didn't leave home. Instead I began writing again, expressing my inner life on paper. I also decided that it would be wise in future to listen to my Voice's advice. From then on, as Harrods was succeeded by Gamages, another large department store, and Gamages by a whole chain of jobs, I made every effort to keep quiet about my other-dimensional experiences.

Just as I was coming up to seventeen, my Voice told me, 'You are ready to begin your work. You can expect it to begin any time. When it does, you must trust it, absolutely.' I was thrilled. I naturally expected whatever it was to start the following week.

It was three years before anything happened.

3

First
Steps

I fully expected that by the age of twenty I would be busy doing whatever I was meant to be doing. Meanwhile I chugged along doing the same kind of jobs, with little happening. It was like waiting for something to come to the boil. I didn't rail against it. The delay taught me that when my Voice tells me something is going to happen I can trust that it will, but I can't impose my own time structure on it; sometimes I just have to wait.

I had a few girlfriends, none of them very serious, but we had fun. I disliked discos and parties, so I picked girlfriends from the minority who were not party-goers. We went to the pictures and the theatre, and took advantage of the lifting of sexual taboos which was one of the nice things about being young in the sixties. It was not just the sexual freedom that I enjoyed, but also the friendliness; my relations with my girlfriends at that time were easy and laid-back.

Another bonus of the sixties was that young men were suddenly allowed to blossom out in amazingly imaginative clothes. I loved wearing bright colours; they made me feel happy. I made the most of the fashions, wearing beads and growing my hair, which was thick and wavy, to shoulder length.

At Gamages for a time I had a girlfriend, Mary. She had a very strict father who only let her go out once a week to attend Gamages' social club, so we had to make the most of her one night out. Her father would pick her up at the end of the evening and she was always worried about being late; one day she told me that if she put a foot wrong he would hit her. I was appalled, particularly when she told me he quite often hit both herself and her mother.

I had a flash of intuition. 'Can you get a look at your birth certificate?' I asked. 'I'm not sure why, but I think it might help you somehow. If you can't find it at home you can look it up at Somerset House.'

Mary went to Somerset House, and was startled to find that the name on the certificate was not that of the man she knew as her father. She confronted her mother, who admitted that her real father had left home when Mary was small. The second man had moved in soon afterwards, and had obviously never taken to Mary. This revelation was quite a shock for her, and she felt let down by her mother for putting her into this situation.

With no loyalties to keep her, Mary left home and moved into a flat with a friend. A week later she announced that she had acquired a new boyfriend. I felt quite hurt at this sudden rejection, especially after the part I had played in gaining her freedom. But I was pleased that at least I had helped her find happiness, and got over it fairly rapidly. This was probably the first time my psychic gifts had been useful to someone else.

When I was twenty things really started to move again for me. My mother introduced me to one of her psychic friends, Sheila Reeves. A large, down-to-earth, very pleasant lady in her forties, she was a natural medium who had seen spirits all her life; her husband, Fred, was a healer.

Sheila ran a weekly spiritualist church in a school hall in Bow. My mother must have told her about some of my experiences, because almost as soon as we met she said, 'Why don't you come along to the church next Tuesday? Just come and see what you think of it.' Spiritualism didn't really attract me, but I instantly agreed – partly out of curiosity, but mainly because I had a very strong feeling that this had to be followed up.

The spiritualist church service was much as I had expected. It was attended largely by middle-aged women, with a scattering of young people. There was a piano for the hymns, and an ordinary table with a cloth over it formed the altar, on which stood a cross within a circle. At the table sat Sheila, as chairperson, and the medium who was to give clairvoyance that evening.

Once everyone was settled Sheila made a welcoming speech, giving us a few words about the nature of spiritualism and its purpose of communicating with those who had passed over and who wanted to help us. There were prayers and hymns, and Sheila gave a reading from spiritualist literature. I found it all rather pseudo-churchy, but decided the best thing was to sit quietly and meditate without letting my impatience take over. I felt there was a good reason for my being there, and I was also curious to know what the medium would do, never having seen one in action.

Claire Sherrick was a local medium whom I hadn't met before. When it was time for her to give clairvoyance she walked up and down among the congregation, tuning into the people for whom she had messages. Most of these messages are, of course, brought through to give comfort to the bereaved. Claire was a very gifted natural medium, and the kind of information she was bringing through obviously came from a genuine source, though I couldn't be sure what that was.

Suddenly she came up to me, and said: 'You must start your healing. You know that already. You also know that there will come a time in the future when you will be known for this, and you will have your own healing centre. But you must start now. You can't ignore what you've been told.' She was right: I knew it already.

At the end of the service, Sheila announced that healing was available for those who wanted it. The regular healers set out chairs for their patients at one end of the hall. Claire came up to me again, and said, 'Come back next week and you can be one of the healers.'

I asked, 'Don't I have to come and learn something first?'

She said, 'I have to trust that you will be given what we've been told you'll be given. You've been told to come and do it, so next week, come! And you can start.'

I looked over at the healing group. People were gathering, both from the congregation and from outside, and sitting down in the chairs. I watched the healers to see what they were doing; some of them were putting their hands over their patient's heads, some waving them around their bodies – they all seemed to be doing something different. I thought that perhaps I would be told what to do.

The intervening week felt like an eternity, as my sense of excitement built up. At last, at long last, something was going to happen: what I had waited for was coming to fruition. How I was going to start healing I still had no idea; I had no instructions, and my Voice didn't speak to me at all that week, despite my pleadings.

The following Tuesday, I turned up at the hall in a state of heightened expectation. Sitting through the prayers and chat was even more tedious, although the clairvoyance, given by a different medium, was fascinating. At the end, I joined the group of healers at the back of the hall. I was given a chair and stood by it with the others, waiting for patients. I thought, 'What do I do? Please help me – don't let me down!' Not a single word did my Voice utter.

The other healers' chairs were already occupied when through the door came a young couple, in their late twenties or early thirties; the woman was walking with great difficulty, almost doubled over, and the man was helping her along. Since I was standing by the only vacant chair, they came straight to me. The poor woman was in such pain she could barely speak.

The man explained, 'My wife has a very bad pro-lapsed disc – it's pressing on a nerve. She's had all the treatments. The only thing left is surgery, which could be dangerous. So I've brought her for healing.'

I said, 'Fine,' hoping my complete lack of confidence wouldn't show, and the husband left us alone together. My patient sat down, with some difficulty. I said, 'OK, just leave it to me.'

I decided to put my hands about her head without touching and – the effect was instantaneous. I felt a huge surge of power go through me. I recognised it as the same energy that had come into me as a child. It felt like being plugged into the mains; I was electrified.

With no decision or control on my part, my right hand started running down the woman's spine while the left hand stayed at her head. She was sitting leaning forward, still doubled over. I felt my hand being almost pushed along her back, until it stopped in the lumbar region. There the energy simply poured out.

After only a few seconds, she suddenly sat up straight, looking amazed, even rather shocked. Her intense, agonising pain was gone. She was able to move and walk. She burst into tears, as people sometimes do when they're overwhelmed. When her husband joined us, he was totally overjoyed. Shortly afterwards she walked out with him, absolutely fine.

As my patient was leaving, my dream of three years earlier suddenly came back to me. Of course, that dream was like an over-dramatised version of the event, but both the dream and this woman's healing showed me the kind of energy available to me. It was a wonderful feeling.

That was my one and only healing that evening. Nobody else came. There weren't that many people needing healing, so regular patients were queuing up for their regular healers. I was a new face, and very young. No one else seemed to have noticed what had happened.

During the week that followed my Voice still didn't speak, but I enjoyed the wonderful feeling of knowing that everything that had always been inside me really was there, that healings like that really were possible. I passed the days in a state of pleasant elation, quite convinced that I was now going to heal everybody.

As I went to work I walked through the streets literally looking for cripples; I could see myself walking up to them and delivering them from their crutches. I didn't, of course; but every time I spotted someone who was obviously in pain or walking with a stick I would think, 'If only you knew that I could cure you! Just with a touch of my hand – wouldn't that be wonderful!'

When I went back to the church the following Tuesday

I put out my chair at the end of the service, fully expecting to perform non-stop miracles. About five people came to me for healing and none of them received anything whatsoever. No energy came; I felt nothing, except a complete and utter blank. I carried on putting my hands in what I thought were the right places, but inside I was sinking into total gloom.

I went home plunged in despondency and had a serious word with my Voice. I said, 'What's going on? I've had this wonderful evidence and now I can't feel any energy.'

And still my Voice said nothing.

I went on feeling miserable for two or three days. Finally, in despair, I decided I would never try healing again.

The moment I made that decision, my Voice came back. It said, 'You really have learnt a lesson.'

I said, 'What lesson?'

The Voice was quite clear. It told me: 'Healing is not always going to be about instant miracles, or curing diseases, and certainly not about you thinking you are there to save everybody. It's not going to be about your ego being bigger than the abilities you've been given. Now you have learnt that lesson, it will return – it will be there for you. You have been given an exceptional gift, as you will see as time goes on. Now you are going to learn how to control and use it.'

That lecture had a profound effect. The words resonated with me deeply, and I felt very much humbled.

So long as one lives in the world, the ego never goes away completely. But what healers have to be aware of and control is that part of the ego that likes to strut around saying, 'How wonderful I am!' I have to acknowledge that I have been given a special gift, that

I am different from a lot of people, and can at times do extraordinary things. But that doesn't automatically make me a wonderful person.

It was on this occasion that my Voice first explained to me how Source Energy had been implanted into me during my illness at the age of five, at a moment when I had briefly died. Later it went into more detail, but it made clear to me now that this had been agreed before my birth.

After that, I became very positive again. I went back to the church service the following week and, although there were no instant miracles, I did get one or two quite good results, with my patients feeling some improvement or relief of pain. I also began to feel that nice rapport that builds up with people when they know that they are beginning the process of healing; they don't walk out cured but they come back next week.

I was still thinking. 'This is it! This is what I've been waiting for.' I expected that in a few months' time this was all I'd be doing. My destiny was now! Of course it wasn't. I had many years of waiting, living and learning ahead of me.

I spent about a year healing with the spiritualist church every Tuesday evening, just allowing myself to learn from experience rather than trying to achieve everything all at once. There were no more miracles. My Voice came occasionally with gentle encouragement, on the lines of 'Don't worry, you're on the right path, just go on with it, just allow it to happen.'

I was learning all the time – about different ailments, and about people's attitudes and expectations. I began to see how these can control a great deal of the results, or non-results, of healing. I discovered that people who go to healers fall into various categories. One or two didn't really want to get better: they were the 'healing groupies' who came back week after week. Then there were a great many whose physical illnesses originated with emotional stress; they were not getting better because at that time conventional medicine treated the disease without addressing the person – an attitude that is fortunately changing now.

There were also the sad cases – those who were desperate because nothing else had worked. All healers get patients who have pursued all the conventional paths in vain, who come for healing as a last resort. By this time the illness has often deteriorated to the point where they are looking for very large miracles. These can happen, but are by no means guaranteed.

My feeling is that healing is a gift which is offered to the individual's Higher Self; it will have some effect on them in some way, but not necessarily in the form of a physical cure. There is no doubt that whatever psychic energy is transferred through healing can bring about physical changes in the body, and I have seen this happen many times. However, if it is going to work, it also has to affect the person's innate belief system and their attitude to their illness.

At the same time, I do not go along with the view of some healers that if healing doesn't work it is the patient's responsibility, even fault. We cannot always know why some people are healed and others are not. In some cases, getting no results from a healer can actually be an important part of the healing process, since patients then take responsibility for themselves and make some inner change. I have, for instance, more than once seen patients who have been prejudiced against orthodox medicine finally recover when they have overcome their fears and undergone surgery.

In addition, healing is always a two-way process.

While some people can benefit from going to more than one healer, there are some who have to find the right person for them. I think this is also true of other therapies: I don't believe that it's particularly homoeopathy, or gem therapy, or grated carrot, that gets people better: it is the combination of the therapist's personal qualities and healing ability that counts, together with the right combination of therapist and patient.

During my year with that church I also learnt quite a lot about healers. A problem with the healing world is that an awful lot of people believe they can do it – and far too many people encourage them – whether or not they have a real gift. You do have to have a gift. I believe that genuine healers and spiritual teachers are born, not made, and their destiny is always clearly shown to them.

Some healers are positive menaces. At one point, later in my career, I was asked to go and see a woman with cancer. When the disease had been diagnosed ten years earlier, she had undergone a mastectomy. Later, the cancer had recurred and she needed further medical treatment. She had been to a healer who told her: 'Don't have any treatment, I will make you better.' By the time I saw her, she had about four weeks to live. There was little I could do for this poor woman except to make her last month more comfortable.

I loved giving healing, whether or not I achieved dramatic results, which on the whole I didn't. One success story that I do remember was a woman who was suffering great discomfort with a serious ear infection, which no one in the medical profession had been able to cure. By the end of the week after her first healing there was a marked improvement, and within three weeks the condition had disappeared. That was very satisfying.

Another case was less immediately successful, but interesting. I used to attend the church service before the healing session. One evening the medium pointed to an elderly woman and said, 'You have been ill.' Then, pointing to me, he went on: 'This young man is your healer. He will cure you. I am getting the figure six – I don't know whether that's six weeks or six months.'

The woman was very highly strung and suffering from all kinds of stress-related problems. I gave her healing regularly, but after a few weeks it became apparent that the medium's statement had been almost too positive. My patient had only heard part of his message and had thought she would be better in six weeks. When she wasn't, she became convinced that it had 'all gone wrong.' I persuaded her to carry on, and it was in fact a good six months before she did finally get better.

As the year went on I began to realise that my future work would not be within any church or organisation, that I did not want to be limited by other people's doctrines. Spiritualism is a religion with a formal, organised doctrine, which imposes certain expectations and behaviour. I have no objection to other people saying prayers and singing hymns, but they are not for me.

I began doing some healing at home – not professionally, but in my spare time. Friends of friends got to know about it, and I went on doing this for many years. I was also exploring a few psychic tools such as Tarot cards. I found that even those friends who laughed at parapsychology would ask me to read their hands or the cards, and I got good results. What I had to tell them was more to do with their characters than their futures, and I could be quite accurate.

Meanwhile, I was growing disenchanted at listening to mediums giving clairvoyance week after week. Mediums are variable in quality and character. There are few genuinely good psychic mediums who pick up information with pinpoint accuracy and know what they're saying. The first two I saw were excellent, producing correct and relevant information from an other-dimensional source. But it seemed to me that, apart from these two, most of the many mediums I saw at this church and others were only minimally psychic. I was already coming to the conclusion that this is the case with 80 per cent of platform mediums. Anyone with a little intuition could probably pick up information from an audience that wants to believe, if only from observing body language.

Week after week, over and over again, I heard the kind of message that goes: 'I'm coming to you, dear, I've got a grandmother, it could be your great-grandmother, but it's on a father vibration, and it says you've been having some trouble but there's lots of light and roses around you.' The mediums who proffer these 'communications' are not fakes who are deliberately conning people; most of them do it for love and don't earn any money from what they do. But I believe that what most mediums are communicating with is an aspect of the person's mind, rather than the whole person. This is why some of the information that comes through even genuine mediums is often so limited and banal.

I would not wish to invalidate the main purpose of communications, which is to tell the living that their loved ones are not lost forever, and are still with them in some form; it can bring great comfort. But it shouldn't prevent the bereaved from completing the grieving process and letting go. A lot of people go to spiritualist churches for this contact week after week and get stuck at that level.

I also found people's desperation to believe rather upsetting. I accepted an invitation one evening to join a circle at the home of one of the church members. We sat round a table with the lights out and candles lit, a prayer was said, and everyone held hands and breathed quietly. As we waited, something in the house creaked. Someone whispered: 'They're here! They're here!'

My Voice said quite loudly in my ear: 'The only thing that's here is their wishes. That's all.'

These nice, sincere people were so strained, so anxious for a spirit visitation, that they saw signs where there were none. Had they relaxed, they might well have had a real visitation, but their very anxiety put pressure on them to believe that something was happening when it wasn't.

In the end, however, it was not my discomfort which led me to leave the spiritualist church. I left because I was told to. One evening my Voice told me: 'That's fine, you have done that part, it is time to move on.'

The spiritualist church had been the focus of the healing side of my life. I thought, 'If I stop, I'll be doing nothing. It's an end; why are you telling me to end?' I was given no instructions as to where I was to move on to, and nothing whatsoever was happening in the rest of my life to indicate a direction. I was faced with the problem I have so often come up against: if I left what I was doing now, I wouldn't be doing anything.

4

Experimenting

I told the people at the church that I had to move on, thanked them for having me and left with no ill feeling on either side. Not long afterwards I met Susan, the first of my girlfriends to play an important role in my life.

None of the girlfriends I had had so far had been really important to me. But with Susan I could share more than fun. The minute I met her I was aware that she had psychic gifts, and when we started talking about our childhoods she told me that she had had similar poltergeist experiences to mine, though not on quite such a grand scale. Within a very short time Susan and I had set up our own experimental psychic circle of two. By now home had finally proved too restricting and I had my own flat, near Shadwell Park on the edge of the Docklands. Here Susan would come to stay at weekends.

It was fun for me to have somebody else to share my explorations with. I sensed that Susan was mediumistic, and quite early on I said, 'Let's see if I can put you into trance.' My knowledge of trance states was partly intuitive and partly based on my experience with the spiritualists. It was very easy. Susan sat opposite me; I said, 'You are feeling very relaxed and are drifting away,' and she was off!

I should add a rider: I do not recommend readers to play about with hypnosis, which can carry risks; there are also ethical considerations. Susan was a willing volunteer, and my interest in putting her into trance was not in any way to control or manipulate her, but to teach her to do it for herself. From then on she was able to put herself into trance whenever she wanted.

With Susan in trance, we tried what I then thought of as astral travelling, a term I would not use now. As I see it, our minds are not confined in space and time, and certainly not within the brain. There is an aspect of our consciousness which is everywhere already, and can thus experience being anywhere within our dimension. So we do not 'travel' on psychic journeys; we can simply open the eyes of our consciousness in another place, and see what's there, instantaneously. It is as if psychics are able to switch on a mental television set linked to broadcasts from all over the universe. But to the conscious human mind, which likes explanations for everything it experiences, it can *feel* like travelling – hence the widespread belief that we have an astral body that travels.

With Susan I started simply. For example, I would rearrange some objects in the next room without telling her, and then ask her to project her mind into that room. The results were instantly quite staggering: she would immediately describe any changes I had made, like putting three cups on the table or moving something from a shelf.

We then experimented further, with Susan mentally viewing different rooms in the house. One day I suggested,

'Why don't you try going through the roof?' We were twenty floors up in a tall block of flats. After a moment she beamed and told me she was floating over London. She really enjoyed it, and gradually gained the confidence to move her awareness further and further out. I would choose places for her to look at that I knew and she didn't. She would describe the wallpaper, the furniture and so on with remarkable accuracy; she was not always 100 per cent correct, but her descriptions were impressive all the same.

I realised that she could be receiving the information telepathically from me, rather than seeing directly with her own mind. So I brought in some friends who would set things up without telling us what they were doing. For example, someone in another room or flat would place three or four playing cards face up on a table, and Susan would read them very accurately at a distance.

We also discovered that she had a talent for reading blindfold, both playing cards and written words. One experiment I spent some time on involved taking ordinary playing cards randomly, placing them on a tray covered with a cloth, and asking Susan to read them. On some days she would get between seven and nine out of ten right – far more than chance. But sometimes it didn't work at all.

Another experiment we tried was a game I had practised on my own: selecting a fairly small object and putting out the thought that at some point we would like it to move. Usually it would move within two or three days, sometimes appearing in another room. Occasionally it would just turn upside down. Of course, it would have been possible for Susan to move the object quite unconsciously as a result of hypnotic suggestion made to her in trance state. I was satisfied that things were moving themselves, but objectively this seemed unprovable. This was brought home to me years later when I started working with scientists and came to realise that, however carefully something is set up, experiments don't provide incontrovertible proof of the paranormal.

What we were doing allowed us both to develop the ability to turn on this kind of psychic mind energy whenever we wanted. We were conducting an exploration of how the mind works on the psychic level. This would be useful to me later on when I would publicly express my views on the paranormal. To speak with any authority, it is preferable to speak from personal experience.

We also practised some healing together; while it was fun to experiment, it was also nice to use our energy for something positive. We did this mainly by sending healing thoughts to those who needed it, and people also came our way for hands-on healing.

Initially we were just the two of us experimenting in my flat. We also went to the occasional spiritualist meeting to observe how clairvoyant energies worked; here we met other young people with similar interests, and we gathered a little group around us.

We were not dabbling but genuinely researching, and throughout I was supported by the powerful certainty that Source Energy had given me permission to do this. I do not advise other people to experiment with the paranormal unless they are very sure of what they are doing. I have always known that I have a powerful inner protection, and have never felt any need to use the protective rituals practised in psychic circles. However, in this kind of work I have always had the inner intention that I will not invite in any negative energies. Energy follows the intention of the user, and the key to protection is therefore one's intention. This can be enhanced, if necessary, by practising rituals such as prayer, or surrounding oneself with white light, and I would never object to anyone using these aids.

I have never been scared of the paranormal. But if people believe, even subconsciously, that there is something to fear, that very belief will be the doorway to invite in negative thought-forms which may affect those present. So for many people it is important to use some kind of protective procedure. Those who are exploring psychic energy, particularly if they are not also pursuing spiritual development, should take into account that this is a very delicate, sensitive area, not to be treated lightly.

This applies particularly to the use of Ouija boards, which have a reputation for attracting unpleasant spirits. We did some experiments with a board, and again I would not recommend everyone to do this. It is not that they necessarily attract spirits or negative thought-forms from outside, though I don't totally rule that out. But a lot of psychic activity goes on within the mind, and opening up the unconscious can unleash repressed aspects of the personality.

The danger with Ouija boards – and I believe one reason they often come up with abusive or threatening messages – is that they allow those involved to make unconscious remarks about others present which they would never say overtly. The group energy will pick up the thoughts of those around the table, and if there is some subconscious ill-will it will come out. Our minds are highly complex and multi-faceted, and participants may allow these usually concealed facets to come to the fore, with the excuse: 'It's not me doing it!' Thus the nastiest things can be expressed such as death threats or other frightening statements, which can be extremely upsetting.

Ouija boards should therefore only be used by people who are highly developed and motivated by integrity, and who know what they are doing. It is possible to receive genuine other-dimensional messages by this method, but it is a very slow way of communicating, and it was not long before Susan and I found faster methods.

The next thing we tried was hypnotic regression – going back in time. The conclusion I came to from my experiments with Susan is that for 98 per cent of the time the mind has an amazing facility to create stories. So in examining the possibility of past lives, you have to create very careful parameters. While reincarnation has a reality, I don't believe that hypnotic regression always takes people back into previous lives, even when they produce plausible stories.

Under hypnosis, the mind is under pressure to come up with something, and the imagination may create scenarios which can then have an existence of their own. Everything the mind creates has some form of reality, albeit often temporary. It may even pick up various bits of genuine historical fact and reassemble them to create a story. For example, Susan might tell me in trance that she was remembering being a peasant girl in 1756. When I questioned her, some of the details she would give were just not possible; often she seemed to be picking up actual facts from different parts of history which could not all have happened in one lifetime.

None of this invalidates hypnotic regression as a therapy, in which a person may enter into a scenario created by their mind to help them solve or shed new light on a problem. Whether or not the actual memory is real, confronting the image of an inner fear or trauma which is affecting one's current life can help to release it, with therapeutic results. (A good account of the many aspects of regression therapy is given by the Jungian psychotherapist Dr Roger Woolger in his book *Other Lives, Other Selves* (Crucible, Thorsons Publishing Group, 1987).) And while I remain very doubtful as to whether hypnotic regression actually brings up memories from past lives, I do believe it allows the mind to move out and pick up genuine facts, which in itself is extraordinary. I also think that most people have mind-links with the past, but hypnosis is only one way of awakening them.

Every now and again we would get a glimmering of something clearly quite different in quality: Susan's whole demeanour would change, indicating to me that she had connected with the actual mind of another person or self. On one occasion she described her life as a German doctor living in Whitechapel, giving his name and the address.

We tried very hard to trace this man. We looked at the streets, and through asking people and researching in libraries we learned that the houses and streets she was describing had really existed, and that a German community had lived there at the time. It was impossible to trace the doctor himself, but in describing this life Susan's whole personality and manner altered as if she had 'become' this man, and she herself felt like a different person.

Once or twice under hypnosis Susan would describe scenes unknown to this planet, and encounters with alien-like beings who seemed to be trying to communicate with her telepathically. She was never frightened during these episodes. I would encourage her to try to get a conversation going, and she would say, 'I can only get a feeling that they're asking me what I want, but there's no language.'

All we could ascertain from these encounters was that

they were not happening on this planet or even in this dimension. Of course, even if we had been given usable information, there would have been no way of proving scientifically that Susan's mind was really in another dimension.

Next we decided to examine the reality of communication with spirits. The first time we tried to make contact, Susan went into trance and lay inert for a while. She then began to gasp a little like a stranded goldfish, as if unable to speak. We gave up after five minutes, but at our third attempt, a day or so later, distinct words started to come through. Speaking slowly in her own voice, Susan announced, 'I'm Jack.'

My ears pricked up. Some friends of my parents had had an only son called Jack who had developed Hodgkin's disease, a form of lymphatic cancer, at around the age of fifteen. Tragically, he died within a couple of years.

I asked some more questions, and it became apparent that I was speaking with this young man. Jack gave us some fairly trivial, simple messages, saying that it was nice to speak to us and so on. I was out of touch with his family by then, and I asked: 'Can you tell us something that would indicate that you really are who you say you are?'

He said, 'Ask about my Dad. I'm really worried – he's got a bad chest infection and it's affecting his heart. He is really quite ill.'

Shortly after this I went to see my mother, who knew about the experiments we were doing. She checked up, and found that the information about Jack's father was completely accurate. I was not concerned at that moment about how it all worked, but I realised that we were getting valid information, as good mediums do, apparently coming from someone I knew.

At our next session, we decided to try to contact a 'guide'. On this occasion, Susan's body went through the kind of physical change that mediums often go through when they allow a guide to speak through them. The body totally relaxes and slumps, and then after a minute or two becomes reanimated.

The change in Susan was quite dramatic, and when she started talking it was in a very deep African voice. The speaker claimed to be a Swahili called Mwomba who was there to guide and help us and tell us how to work. His voice was very theatrical – 'Me Mwomba!' – which I found rather unconvincing, and I could not really accept that we were in touch with the spirit of a Swahili.

Mwomba told us he found it hard to speak, and that Susan should write instead. That began a long phase of automatic writing. When Mwomba came through Susan would hold the pen upright in her fist and fill many pages with huge, heavy letters. We conversed in this way for several weeks.

The important question to ask in evaluating this kind of experience is 'What does the information tell us!' I haven't kept Mwomba's writings because when I looked at them later I realised that he had said nothing of any real value. His communications consisted of very simple, homespun philosophy, sometimes at the level of, 'Be sure to protect yourself, it's cold today.' You don't need someone from another dimension to tell you to wrap up warmly. When I compared this kind of advice with the profound information and guidance I sometimes got from my own Voice, I wondered why someone purporting to be a guide was so lacking in depth.

One notable feature was that there was a lovely atmosphere in the room when Mwomba was speaking. But whenever I asked specific questions about, for example, where Mwomba was, I never got a straight answer. In addition, Susan herself had good insights and was better informed when she was not taken over by Mwomba than when she was.

I am satisfied that Susan was not faking anything; she had no reason to. But, as with hypnotic regression, I believe that the mind has a tendency to dramatise information. I believe that what was speaking through her was a constructed piece of mind energy, adopting a persona called Mwomba; possibly a real Swahili called Mwomba had once existed. Without this identity, Susan would simply have been contacting unformed energy. Her unconscious mind had tapped into a particular image to give this formless energy a personality which she could allow to speak through her.

Similarly, when a 'spirit guide' speaks through a medium, the personality of the guide may quite often be a construct that allows the medium to relay information from the vast store of psychic information to which their mind has access. The medium may actually be in touch at some level with the mind of a real person. What I question is whether the complete personality is really coming back. This was the case with our next communicator.

One day, Susan was writing in Mwomba's hand when suddenly the writing changed completely. She wrote: 'I have come to talk to you and will be part of your guidance from now on.' We couldn't make out the signature, which was very elaborate and squirly.

I said, 'Who are you?'

Susan's hand wrote, 'I am a poet.'

I asked the communicator to write some poetry, and he did – some very lovely poetry. Everything he wrote was in a charming, elegant, educated English which flowed beautifully.

Mostly through this writing, and sometimes speaking aloud through Susan, the poet began to give us rather more profound information than that produced by Mwomba. The messages were often on a practical level: 'We will try to help you with your experiments, and change the energy to help you,' and so on. And the poems really were good. (Unfortunately I no longer have them, since I gave them to Susan when she eventually moved abroad.)

We had some dialogue with this poet almost every day for several weeks. One day I said: 'You keep signing, but we can't read your signature. Will you tell us who you are?'

He spelt out, 'Yes, I'm Shelley.'

I was very fond of Shelley's poetry and had a book of his works in my flat. I hadn't recognised any of the verses he had given us so far; they were Shelley-ish, though perhaps more romantic than his usual style.

So I said, 'Fine. If you're Shelley, write me a piece of your poetry.'

He immediately produced a poem, which I found in my book of Shelley's works.

I became convinced that whatever we were in touch with was certainly something to do with the mind of Shelley, or some aspect of his mind, linked with me perhaps through my love of his poetry. He talked beautifully and elegantly, sometimes making jokey remarks like: 'I only wish I could enjoy a glass of wine again.' He even mentioned the name of a wine which we found existed in Shelley's lifetime. But to me, nothing that he said or wrote convinced me that we were actually talking to Percy Bysshe Shelley.

There was one fascinating detail: when he was writing through her Susan could hear his voice, and I asked what it sounded like. She said, 'Well, it's odd, because it's rather high and squeaky.' We went to a library and found a biography which described his voice as being rather high and squeaky.

I still reserved judgment. I felt we could be talking with an aspect or fragment of the mind of Shelley as it was during his lifetime: I was still not sure that we were talking to the whole person. If Shelley had been communicating as a whole being, this would have included his spiritual development after death; he would no longer have been as he was in life, but Shelley-plus.

A counter-argument might be that he had come back as he was in his lifetime so that we could recognise him. But if you are looking for spiritual truths or new information about the psychic, it is important to avoid being so taken up with the personality of the speaker that you do not examine the content of what is said. 'Shelley' said nothing to indicate that the information was moving me, or him, or Susan, forward in any way.

At the time I only understood that what we were communicating with, while fascinating, could not be the whole being. This understanding was enhanced when we came to ask questions which 'Shelley' evaded or left unanswered. I might say: 'Tell me more about your life, give me chapter and verse about things I can go and look up.' 'Shelley' would reply, 'I am not wasting my time with that.'

All this work went on over quite a long period, sometimes with just the two of us and sometimes with our friends. They joined us as a group to do healing, and we experimented with clairvoyance and psychometry, and with getting objects to move by thought. One evening we had an apport: a small silver ring simply appeared on the carpet in the middle of the floor round which we were all sitting. When we picked it up it was warm; it literally glowed for a while, as if it had been somewhere hot.

None of what we learned came from books. Any guidance came from my Voice, always in a very internal, undramatic way. It was as if it had presented me with a playroom full of toys and told me to play. I was given no clear instructions about, for example, whether we were talking to real spirits: I had to work these things out for myself.

I think the main purpose of all of this, for me anyway, was to consolidate the physical energy that had returned to me together with what is called mental mediumship. It was also part of a process of learning how these things are perceived by others, and how they actually work. I was beginning to develop my own ideas about how to reinterpret these phenomena. A lot of my learning has been by doing rather than sitting down quietly and being taught.

There was another area in which I had some serious learning to do. Susan had moved into my flat after the first few months. Because we worked and lived together, I believed quite sincerely for a time that our relationship must have been made in heaven, that we must have met for a purpose, and that we would always be together and work together.

After about two years it came as a nasty shock when the blinkers were removed. It suddenly became obvious to us both that we no longer had a relationship. It just wasn't there. The work was fascinating, the energy was fascinating, but we wanted quite different things.

Until very recently all my relationships have suffered from the fact that, throughout my life, the only really important thing has been my work. Since childhood I had been driven by the absolute conviction that there was something I must work towards, and that this must be paramount. Consequently I behaved as though I expected any woman in my life to devote herself utterly to me, without asking for anything in return. I am told that some men expect this anyway; with me it was worse because my purpose always took priority.

My attitude was: 'This is what I do; if you want to live with me you support it. You come one rung down the ladder, on the rung below the work.' This attitude was not born out of sexism; I have always believed in men and women having totally equal rights. Had I been sharing my flat with a man, it would have been the same. I was the genius; the other person's role was not to bother me with trivia. From time to time my friends have complained that I give more importance to the driving force within me than to my friendships. Luckily, they are still my friends.

There have been women throughout history crazy enough to agree to be Mozart's wife, as it were – to say, 'You're a creative genius, so I will serve you for the rest of my life.' They were the products of a certain kind of society, and a lot of women have suffered a great deal because of it. Of course the work is important, but it's important to bring it into your life in such a way that your private life works too.

Meanwhile, my shared life with Susan wasn't working; there was no deep emotional tie to bind us. For her, psychic experimentation was a relatively minor interest. She was tired of being expected to sit blindfold reading cards. She wanted other things, like children and a family life – all of which horrified me!

We began to argue regularly – one evening she threw my dinner at me. I said I was too busy with some creative work to come to the table and eat what she'd just cooked, so she said, 'Have it now, then!' Not at that time a vegetarian, I found myself covered in steak, chips and peas. Susan clearly saw me as totally self-centred. My attitude was one of simple astonishment that she didn't appreciate the importance of what I was doing – work that I felt would ultimately change people's view of the world.

Finally we agreed to have a break from each other, and Susan went to stay with her family while we sorted things out. She never came back. After a couple of heart-rending telephone conversations and an exchange of several letters it was clear that we would not get together again. We went our own ways, not amicably at first, though later we became friendly. Eventually Susan married an American and went to live in the USA.

I was alone again, which for a time wasn't a problem. I spent a year on my own, healing people in my spare time and reading a great deal – something I hadn't done before. Around this time I trained to become a Samaritan, and worked with them as a volunteer for about six months. Their policy is to listen to callers and allow them to express their feelings without making judgments, giving advice or interfering in any way; the training would benefit any healer who likes to tell their patients what to do, rather than empowering them to work out their own problems.

The feeling that I was here for a purpose never left me. It was almost obsessive; I was beginning to feel that I had to sacrifice everything, including relationships, because of what I was here for. It was extraordinarily powerful knowing that whatever happened, however miserable life was, however much I disliked my job – which I usually did – and no matter what was going wrong, I only had to stick it out because ultimately I would be given whatever I was here to do. But it was taking so long!

At one point I began saying to my Voice, 'If I have a special purpose, please do something about it, or I'll be dead before it happens!' I got no reply.

Throughout the period of waiting I continued to work at various jobs, enjoying the company of a series of girlfriends, and giving healing in my spare time. It was nearly ten years before anything of note happened in my life. When it did, it took the form of a relationship which was more important than any I had ever had.

5

Metamorphosis

During my adult life the Source Energy which has always been a part of me has gradually been expanding to become the dominant part, just as the butterfly grows invisibly within the hard shell of the pupa, ultimately to emerge as a totally different creature. Up to and during my time with Susan I had been feeding like the caterpillar, absorbing information and learning all I could. Then I entered the pupal stage, and I remained a pupa for a long time.

The pupa looks lifeless, but within the shell the body of the caterpillar completely liquifies, gradually to re-form as a butterfly. Similarly, while nothing much was happening in my external life, internally I was re-forming. Although I was not visiting gurus or listening to spiritual teachers, somewhere inside me I was learning, acquiring vast amounts of knowledge, in my own way. But it was happening so internally that none of this knowledge could become conscious until the time was ripe.

Unlike the butterfly, my metamorphosis was to take

many, many years. And as far as I know, the butterfly experiences no conflict between its old and new self. In my own case I have had to learn to balance my human side, my emotional side, with Source Energy which is beyond emotion. At times this has been far from comfortable.

In my late twenties and early thirties I was once again in the wilderness. Despite having a certain amount of fun I felt constantly on the edge of society, although I just wanted to be normal. I never completely lost my intuition and psychic abilities and I never totally lost contact with my Voice, even though it was not there all the time. I never stopped healing. But I began to resent the feeling of having been chosen, of having to be different, with very little to show for it and no full understanding of why.

Locked up in my pupa phase, there were times when I would erupt into impatience, and during my early thirties I went through a stage of semi-rebellion. I would ask my Voice: 'Why do I have to do this? Why do I know I've got a destiny, when years go by and nothing seems to happen?'

Looking back, it seems that one reason for the waiting was that, in order to work as I do now, I had first to reach certain points in my purely human development. I had to spend time finding out about myself, and face up to my personal problems and behaviour.

The catalyst for this was Chris. My relationship with her marks what I can think of as the beginning of my emergence from the pupa. For the butterfly this takes a few hours, and once its wings are dry it can fly. My emergence has taken several years. First I had to face the very real conflict between my emotional life and the work, which was not to be resolved for a long time. With Chris I was, so to speak, drying my wings.

The one extra-mural activity I had taken up with Susan was amateur dramatics, which made a break from all our psychic exploring. A group of friends who met at a social club in South London asked me to produce a music-hall show for charity. We needed a pianist and I was put in touch with Chris, who played the piano and taught it to adults. Her main job was being a schoolteacher – a brilliant one, I later discovered, when I had an opportunity see her at work.

At the time we met she was married with a small daughter. With her slightly gypsyish look, long brown hair and colourful, unconventional clothes I found her very striking, and she came across as a free spirit. But we didn't particularly like each other at first, and it certainly didn't occur to me that she was going to be of major importance in my life. She was several years older than me, and I think she found me arrogant and conceited.

She agreed to play for our show, and during the production we became quite friendly. I admired her tolerant, peaceable approach to life. She had spent a year in India teaching Tibetan refugees and, although not a practising Buddhist, she had a basically Buddhist attitude. Despite the stresses of being a working mother, she had a great serenity about her.

I didn't see her for a couple of years, when I needed her help again with another show. By now she had a second daughter, but her marriage was running into difficulties. Although we renewed our friendship, it was to be years before that friendship flowered into love.

In the early 1980s I was working for a big firm of chartered accountants, and in serious danger of becoming a worldly success. Starting out as a filing clerk, I had been rapidly promoted to assistant administrative manager for London, a job entitling me to an office and half a secretary. (I always said that the manager I shared her with got the half that worked; my half had the tea-breaks, and I learned to type with two fingers.) Eventually I realised that I was at risk of being made manager, with a secure job for life, a suit, a tie and a pension, and I left.

Meanwhile, my friendship with Chris had been developing over time into something much deeper. This slow, long process of falling in love was something I had never experienced before. Chris was not just an attractive woman, but a beautiful soul with a tolerance that the world needs, and with a capacity for giving that I have rarely seen. I loved her attitude to life, her inner freedom, the profound love of music which we shared. I loved the way she managed to enjoy life and find pleasure in it, even when circumstances were difficult.

It slowly dawned on me that I was only enjoying myself when Chris was around. I found myself responding to her moods, caring about her feelings and wishing I could help her. I don't usually hide my feelings when attracted to someone but, quite unusually for me, I knew it would be inappropriate to say anything so long as she was married.

Eventually, Chris and her husband agreed to separate, and he moved out. Now that she was at least nominally free I could broach the subject of us, but she was very hesitant about entering another relationship. At first I took a flat near her house, and visited her every day. Our love grew in the shadow of her former marriage. Her ex-husband visited the children regularly, and I did not move in until after he remarried.

Chris and I were together for nearly ten years. For me it was a time of learning and a time of healing. With her I began to express feelings I must have been harbouring unconsciously for years, and eventually started to come to terms with them. It was quite scary to let out so much emotion; this was something I had never done before.

For the first time I was able to feel and express a very real and deep love for another person. At the same time, this love brought up something quite new to me: a very powerful, almost paranoid fear of being deserted, which I think must have stemmed from the time when I was left in hospital as a child. During the first year or two I lived in constant fear that our relationship was going to end, and for a time I didn't want to do anything or go anywhere without her. Chris finally began to feel exasperated, and made it clear that I was being too dependent. (I was also being unfair, since I valued my own space very highly and could get quite annoyed if I felt it was invaded.)

With Chris I learned a lot about myself, including the fact that, while I expect to have things my own way, other people may legitimately have another point of view. Even today, when it comes to my work, things have to be just as I want them, because my work is important to me. Chris was no exception: I expected her to fit into the way I wanted things. But since she was strong, she would fight back.

At first, I was terrified of arguments. If my parents had ever had any rows I knew nothing about them. I did not understand that expressing anger with someone didn't mean that you had stopped loving them, and for quite a while I was afraid that if I lost my temper I might lose Chris. But when we had our first major row it was liberating for both of us, and afterwards I had not lost Chris.

I have felt it important to write about the personal side of my life because, so often in the biographies of spiritual teachers and healers, personal problems are glossed over.

Historically, we are told little about the private lives of people with my kind of gifts. The biographies of saints and healers are sanitised so that we only hear about their goodness; yet their emotional lives must have included problems and conflicts.

The only way in which the Source can influence this planet is through human beings like myself, which means that it has to work through fallible human bodies and emotions. When the Source comes into a human body, it agrees to take part in the energy of the human dimension. Nobody who does spiritual work can avoid emotional struggles. Jesus must have gone through them, and so must the Buddha. I don't believe they conquered them easily: more than that, they may on occasions have failed to conquer them, although history has cleaned that up.

Some holy people have dealt with the problem of their humanity by removing themselves from the world, but that is not a solution for everyone. When I am totally working with Source Energy, when I am healing or channelling, emotions don't enter into it. There is compassion, but it is impersonal. By contrast, in my everyday life I couldn't have human relationships if I didn't have human emotions. I could only avoid them by becoming a hermit, in which case I wouldn't reach the people I want to reach. My path has had to involve normal, human experience.

Chris and I lived happily together for some years. I know now that through all this time Source Energy was working within me, but it was not at a conscious level. I was still not clear about my purpose and, apart from some healing in my spare time, I was doing little to pursue this side of my life. Chris was not involved in my healing or psychic interests, and we wanted to do something together outside work.

After leaving the accountancy firm, I decided that I needed a job that would give me more free time to spend with her, and put the thought out that if such a job existed I would find it. Shortly afterwards I saw an advertisement for a night-time co-ordinator with a security firm, to work one week in three. I went for an interview with the absolute certainty that I would get the job, and was offered it on the spot.

Chris and I took advantage of my daytime freedom to join an afternoon singing class at Morley College in South London – Rita Godfrey's 'Enjoy Your Voice'. We both gained an enormous amount from these sessions. We enjoyed singing, but there was more to it than that. When I first encountered Rita Godfrey I thought she was a lovely person: she radiated something special.

Once we started going to her classes I realised she was doing much more than teaching singing – something in fact akin to what I was doing in healing, though she was working in a different way and with a different energy. As well as teaching the technical side of voice production, she was connecting people with sound as a spiritual force. Like Chris, Rita is a very giving person; I was fascinated with her as someone with huge potential musical talents that remained unexplored because she was giving so much to others. She was healing, and teaching people to heal themselves, by expanding their spiritual beings through sound.

It had occasionally crossed my mind that I would like to take up music professionally, and this feeling was revived now. I could never have been a concert pianist, but I could play the piano and the guitar pretty well by ear, and could envisage myself singing to my own accompaniment. I enjoy performing; during my days of amateur dramatics I discovered that when I sang sad songs to my guitar I had the ability to move people to tears – not because I had a wonderful voice, but because I wasn't afraid to express feelings. This, too, has been a part of my spiritual training: when I speak to large groups, audiences don't scare me.

Chris and I sang now and again at small concerts at Morley and elsewhere, and I directed another Victorian-style music-hall show for charity. I found that I knew intuitively how all the old songs should sound. Source Energy enables me to attune to other dimensions of time, and to re-create the atmosphere. Also, I had felt a connection with the music hall since childhood. When I was about eight I heard on the radio an old recording of Marie Lloyd singing one of her songs; I immediately burst into tears and cried all the way through. I could not explain why; I was simply overwhelmed by an enormous sadness.

During our own show, Chris displayed amazing talents. She not only played the piano, but performed music hall songs with great gusto and professionalism. She had the audience in the palm of her hand.

It was while I was living with Chris that my spiritual work began to revive and flower. During this time she was to give me every support, but this very revival was to sow the seeds of our breaking up because once again my work became paramount. Neither of us foresaw this at the time. It began in 1986, when an incident at work jolted me forward on my path.

The job with the burglar alarm company was suiting me well. The work was undemanding; all I had to do was to contact the police and engineers if an alarm came in. There were always two of us on night shift, and when it got quiet round about eleven we could – quite against the rules – take turns to get three hours' sleep. I would sleep for another five or six hours when

I got home, and be sufficiently restored to enjoy my time off.

At work I became friendly with a young man called Mark, one of the day workers. He sometimes did overtime at night, and we would get chatting. Mark had a normal seventeen-year-old's interest in sports and the like, but he was also curious about the paranormal. We talked about the subject quite often and he knew I was psychic, though I didn't go into great detail about my experiences.

One evening he asked, not very seriously, 'Can you communicate with dead people? I'm fascinated by that.'

I said, 'I can, if they are willing.'

At that very instant a man appeared beside Mark. Mark saw nothing, but to me he looked solid and real: he was elderly, slightly bent, and dressed in an old jacket and baggy trousers. He told me: 'I'm Mark's grandfather, my name's William. Why don't you tell him that?' As he spoke, I became aware that he had a lame leg.

When I told Mark what I was seeing and hearing, his mouth literally fell open. He said, 'I don't believe it! I'm going to have to check this, because my grandfather did limp, but I don't know his first name – he died too long ago.'

He immediately phoned his mother from the office, and she confirmed that her father's name had been William. William gave me some more facts about himself, and I ended up giving Mark's mother a clairvoyant reading over the phone, including information about her circumstances and worries which intrigued and quite impressed her.

I had not had such a three-dimensional visitation since my childhood meeting with Fred. I felt I was having a genuine conversation with a real person. Our talk didn't last very long, but it was not fragmented as 'spirit communications' often are; I could ask William questions and receive straight answers, and the information he asked me to pass on was relevant.

When I got home I told Chris about it, somewhat tentatively; I trusted her totally, but it had become ingrained in me to be careful what I said. In the past people had often suddenly altered their view of me after such revelations, and a part of me was still fearful of rejection. But I need not have worried; Chris took it in her stride.

The William incident was like the starting signal for me to get moving again. As well as continuing healing I had sat in various circles, and had occasionally talked with my Voice – though it had been mostly silent of late. Now I knew I had to take some kind of action and move towards something new.

As so often in my life, an apparent 'coincidence' at just the right time showed me where to go next. A couple of weeks later I happened to read a newspaper article about the paranormal which mentioned the celebrated medium Ivy Northage; a highly respected spiritualist, she has for many years been channelling a Chinese spirit teacher called Chan. The article also mentioned that she ran a training course in mediumship at the College of Psychic Studies.

The minute I read the article I knew I had to telephone the College. I rang them and explained that I had been compelled to call because psychic things had been happening in my life. The receptionist told me that Ivy Northage was holding interviews for her course the following week, and suggested I went along.

The night before my interview my Voice came with the instruction: 'Whatever you know already, whatever you are aware of, whatever you have done, do not use it. Go to the interview as a pupil, not as somebody who thinks he knows it all.' It was an enormous relief to have this direct contact with my Voice after quite a barren time: at this moment I knew that my long period of waiting was over. Without questioning the reasons, I took my Voice's advice – which was just as well, or I would never have got past the front door with Ivy.

When I arrived for my interview I was greeted warmly by a beautiful, white-haired lady, smartly dressed, with a lovely, welcoming smile: Ivy comes across initially as everyone's favourite grandmother. (I soon discovered that the velvet glove enclosed a fist of steel.) She gave off a kind of shining energy – the effect, I believe, of her total commitment and service to her spiritual guides. With her was her devoted assistant Janet Orman.

Remembering my Voice's instructions, I kept my statements brief and simple; I didn't mention my healing activities or tell her anything about my childhood. I think Ivy had decided to accept me before I opened my mouth. She made sure that I was willing to give the time and commitment to studying and then told me, 'I'll have you in my group, but you'll have to start with the beginners.'

With some trepidation I told Chris I would be attending Ivy's classes. It was, I fear, typical of me that I went to the interview first and then presented her with the *fait accompli*. In fact she raised no objections, though she could not really see the value of studying mediumship. I myself was not totally sure why the Source wanted me to do it, but I knew that there must be a reason.

6

Emergence

A month after my interview I duly turned up at the College of Psychic Studies, which was to play an important role in my life. The College is an educational charity, set up as a non-denominational body open to seekers of the spiritual and psychic truth. It offers public lectures, courses and private sittings with a variety of mediums and psychics; it also has a large and excellent reference library.

The Ivy Northage School of Mediumship, though not part of the College, had an arrangement to use its premises. The School was run on hierarchical lines; during the three-year course students were taken through a series of grades which could eventually lead to a certificate in mediumship if Ivy considered them worthy of it.

The beginners' group was taken by Janet Orman, whom I liked very much. Earlier in her life she had given up her personal psychic development to assist Ivy and teach in the school. Ivy herself was held in very great reverence, almost fear, by her students and colleagues. She knew that her method worked, and allowed no one to deviate from it. She was always very good to me and gave me a lot of encouragement.

With Janet we studied the chakras, the psychic energy centres of the body. We learned the functions of each one, and spent weeks simply learning how to open them to receive psychic information, and how to close them down again when we had finished. This is a very mechanical method of working, but it has its advantages. Many budding psychics don't actually *want* to switch off; they can get quite high on their gifts, and enjoy telling people what they can see and hear whether or not they are invited to. This can be very intrusive. Before describing people's guides or launching into spontaneous clairvoyance, psychics should be quite sure that the information will be welcome.

A structured method such as Ivy's gives developing psychics strong boundaries, and teaches them to be disciplined about their use of energy. In addition, to those who follow the chakra system the closing down of the energy centres at the end of a healing or psychic session can provide a useful safeguard against being open to negative energies.

I found the beginners' class very slow, and had to sit on my impatience. But I stayed with it because my Voice told me to. I was being told, 'You have to learn this – there is a reason. Don't think there is nothing to be gained from going back to the beginning.'

After three months I was moved into a class run by Sheila Häve, one of the College mediums, who was being tried out as a teacher. She quickly recognised that I had something quite powerful and encouraged me to extend my abilities beyond the normal syllabus. In Sheila's class my energy came to life again, and

I started getting clairvoyance and psychic communications.

With Sheila we studied psychometry, a means of gathering information about someone by holding an object they have owned for a long time. The theory is that people's energies are recorded in their possessions – watches, rings and so on – which can then be 'read' by handling them. Psychometry can enable you to be extraordinarily accurate about someone's personality and habits; it often tells people what they already know, but it can highlight problems they are perhaps not facing.

We would read objects that had been placed in the middle of the group without knowing whose they were, and I turned out to be very good at it. I remember on one occasion reading a watch belonging to a man. I described his girlfriend, who wasn't English, and told him correctly that his relationship with her was fairly new. I saw and described them sitting in a bar somewhere which I thought was near Spain; it turned out to be Gibraltar. I even hummed the tune that was being played in the bar. Then I told him that he and his girlfriend had shared an extraordinary psychic experience which they had told no one about. When I had finished, he said, 'You must have been following me around!'

It was another matter when people tried to read objects belonging to me. The Source Energy within me makes it very difficult for most psychics to tap into me, and I have had some wildly inaccurate readings in my career. I have only ever met one medium who gave me an accurate sitting from beginning to end. Two people have tried to give readings of my energy system, one through radionics and one through aura reading; both told me that they could not find my energy centres, and that I must be either dead or an alien!

After a few weeks, Sheila was suddenly removed – because, it was rumoured, she had stepped outside the structure of Ivy's course. I was swiftly moved up to the next level, taught by Roger Stone, who at that time was Ivy's heir apparent; he had worked with her for many years and became a good friend of mine. As Ivy's students were elevated to the group which Roger taught (the one below Ivy's), they were sent out to churches to give clairvoyance and mediumship to the public from the platform. This was normally during the third year of training, but Roger recognised that I had gifts and unbeknownst to Ivy got me one or two bookings before my third year – had she found out she might have expelled me.

I did wonder at times why I was having to go through Ivy's very structured system of learning, all the time sitting on my own inner knowledge. One thing that this experience brought home to me was that structures can be both beneficial and imprisoning. People can go through a system like Ivy's and learn to be very competent mediums, but the system itself traps them within the limits of competence.

Of course, I benefited in some purely practical ways. I learned some self-discipline, which I had lacked until then, in the use of my own psychic abilities. I learned when to use my energy and when not to, and how to look after myself, all of which I really value. I gained useful experience of working with people, and of standing on numberless platforms, to give clairvoyance. At the time, although I did not need to, I always followed Ivy's method of contacting all the chakras to receive each piece of clairvoyant information, a process we eventually learned to go through very speedily.

Ivy ensured that her students were as accurate as possible. Giving clairvoyance can be rather like playing charades: the medium will see an image and hear a voice, and then perhaps be given symbolic pictures. From these composite clues you have to interpret something meaningful to the person addressed. It is very easy for a psychic who is badly trained, or who feels compelled to come up with answers, to misinterpret these clues. Since their interpretations can have an influence on the sitter's emotional or practical life, this is a big responsibility. Ivy always taught that if you didn't know what something meant, you should keep quiet about it.

This also raised a question, one of many that came up for me during Ivy's classes: if spirits can give clues – first names and so on – why on earth can't they speak fluently and give their information in a straightforward fashion? Why go through an elaborate charade? The medium's usual explanation is: 'The spirit world uses what is there.'

My own conclusion is that mediums may be tuning in not to the fully formed minds of individuals, but to fragments of mind arriving in bits and pieces, and that this is more often than not what happens during mediumistic clairvoyance. Some clairvoyance is purely telepathic. I have on occasion been able to give total strangers their names and addresses, the colour of their front doors and other pieces of personal information, all absolutely accurately. This is valid evidence that psychic energy exists, but it has nothing whatsoever to do with spirits.

Whether I was actually in touch with 'spirits' or not, I could reach out my mind and produce the correct names and accurate descriptions of people's dead relatives. I was less sure whether the information I was passing on actually came from the 'spirit world'. Sometimes I knew I was in touch with a thinking personality, as I had been with Mark's grandfather. More often, I believe, I was simply retrieving pieces of information from some kind of database of thought.

In fact, even when a complete personality 'comes through' I don't necessarily regard this as a spirit coming back to this plane. Spirits don't have to 'come back' in the sense of moving through spatial dimensions to reach a medium's mind. At the time of communication the medium views just that part of the 'spirit's' mind that formed their personality. Because consciousness cannot die, all thoughts are potentially accessible; but that does not necessarily prove that one is communicating with a whole person.

I also believe that sometimes mediums are locating only the part of the mind of the dead person that exists within the mind of the sitter. What comes through has the personality of the person as they were in life, but no more than that. In other words, the 'spirit' is no wiser than any ordinary living person who is not in touch with their higher consciousness.

Occasionally that level can be transcended, and the medium is aware of a very powerful presence which means that they are in touch with the *whole* person. When 'spirit' messages come from the complete personality, including the higher consciousness, the communication has a totally different quality. The conversation flows as if the person is really there, and truly helpful advice and guidance may be given. However, this may not be what the sitter wants to hear.

Most people who go to spiritualist mediums are seeking comfort, and some return to the same church year after year to hear the same comforting but mundane messages. Clairvoyance from mediums and psychics can be comforting and sometimes useful, but this should not be an excuse for sitters not to change, or to continue to look to dead relatives for help without letting them go. After death we have the potential to become our full selves, in touch with all the aspects of our minds which we may have been unaware of in life, including our higher consciousness. Death can be a gateway to infinite knowledge and infinite dimensions, and no one should be held back from moving on.

After my father's death I had one or two conversations with him which helped us both to clear up some unresolved issues. I saw him briefly, but mainly felt his presence and that he wanted to talk with me. Although he had often claimed to disbelieve in an afterlife, in his last year he admitted that he had changed his mind. I suspect that after death it was still very difficult for him to make the transition between his previous expectations and the potential for discovering and opening up to other, unknown parts of his mind and spirit.

I said the usual things – that I hoped he was all right and happy and so on. He was concerned about my mother, who was very upset; I also understood that he realised there was a lot for him to learn. We hadn't always got on, and I had the impression that he thought we should try to become closer now. I didn't want him held back by unfinished business. I told him he didn't have to come back to visit me; that if there were things for him to discover, this was important and I was happy for him to move forward.

The spiritualist view of the afterlife is actually severely limited. Its concept of the next world is of a place much like here but brighter and happier, with tea and biscuits, where we carry on much as before. Of course all forms of religion, including the Catholic Church and the Church of England, have similarly constructed afterlives in keeping with their doctrines. This is why people have quite genuine near-death experiences which fit the particular doctrines in which they have been brought up. But this is a denial of the multi-dimensionality of the mind.

In my view spiritualism and other religious doctrines place a restriction on the mind's potential to explore beyond the physical body. This could possibly limit the experience of the mind after death, rather than expanding it. I have no doubt that a spirit world exists, where people continue to have experiences. However it is simply another dimension, created by a belief system. In order to progress to the full spiritual potential that lies beyond, it is necessary to go beyond this comfortable structure and move on.

My first Ivy-approved attempt at public clairvoyance was at the spiritualist church at Pembridge Place in West London, where I later got married; it is one of the very few spiritualist churches in which I have really felt comfortable. It was here that members of Ivy's and Roger's groups were invited to demonstrate their stage of development to a spiritualist congregation. I mounted the platform, opened myself up as taught by Ivy and was immediately drawn to a young man in glasses. When I did clairvoyance in public, it was as if the person I had to speak to was somehow magnified: the face would appear to come up to me out of the crowd. I went up to this chap and said, 'I have your grandfather here, and he tells me that you are an extremely clever person, but your one big problem is that you argue with everybody.'

'No, I don't!' he said, and the whole place erupted into laughter.

I said, 'I don't wish to be offensive, but he's telling me that you always argue for the sake of it, whether or not you believe in your argument.'

'No, I don't!' he said.

A friend of his sitting behind him was nodding and

mouthing, 'Yes, he does!' She was killing herself with laughter.

During the next ten minutes I continued to give him information, and he continued to argue with every single statement I made. That was a real baptism of fire.

Going round the churches is a hard training ground for developing mediums. Over the years I have met many mediums who are astonished that when visiting churches there is nowhere for them to relax and meditate. Some churches, however, are wonderful; they understand that mediumship involves sensitivity, and offer you a quiet room where you can gather yourself in peace beforehand. Similarly I did meet some really nice, generous, thoughtful people. But on the other hand there are many spiritualist churches which are strongly committee-based, and as in any organisation some committee members appear to exist for the purpose of feeding their own self-importance rather than for the greater good.

Once, giving clairvoyance in a church, I was drawn to a woman in the congregation whom I realised had a frozen shoulder. I said, 'Come up here, and it'll be cured' (not something I would guarantee without an absolute sense of certainty). I gave her healing, and she returned happily to her seat with her shoulder healed. But some of the committee members were less appreciative. They told me, 'You're not here to do healing, you're here to do clairvoyance!'

Probably the most important reason for my going through Ivy's training was that it gave me the opportunity to study a particular belief system thoroughly from the inside, and to draw my own conclusions as to what was really going on. Thinking these things through while experiencing them at first hand enabled me eventually to speak about them with some authority. Aspects of mediumship and spiritualism, such as the nature of the spirit world, life after death and reincarnation, have all been rethought for me through the channelling I developed after leaving Ivy. But I had to learn about the traditional viewpoint first.

The teaching I subsequently developed through channelling puts systems like spiritualism into a different perspective. For me, channelling means directly linking with and speaking from the Source, which is very different from the channelling that involves spirit guides speaking through mediums.

Very much later I received the understanding that the Universe we are in, including other dimensions, is contained within a Vortex which we perceive as infinite, but which is in fact relatively limited. It contains a store of information which is vast but also limited – the database of mind I have described, from which is drawn the kind of information that most mediums produce.

It is also possible to communicate with and channel minds from outside this Vortex, the true infinity where Source Energy has its being, and where my Voice comes from. Some channels, as well as avatars like Sai Baba and other spiritual teachers, are also in touch with minds outside the Vortex. There is an enormous difference between these minds and the Red Eagles and White Feathers who 'guide' so many mediums from within the confines of the Vortex. I do not dismiss these as totally valueless, but the time has come when we need communication from outside the Vortex in order to understand our future evolution.

By mid-1987, in the second of my three years undergoing Ivy Northage's training, my life had become uncomfortably full. My relationship with Chris was very creative, but there was little time for it. I was doing the night job, my development in Ivy's group was going well, and I was also going out nearly every week to spiritualist churches to give healing and clairvoyance from the platform. So my physical energy was constantly being drawn on without being replenished – a trap into which many healers and psychics fall.

Although I sometimes get very tired, I have never as a rule found it difficult to restore my energy. But after more than a year of juggling this life, I realised that although the job had served a purpose it was also wearing me down. The disruption to my sleeping pattern was beginning to take its toll; it was getting harder and harder to relax, and harder and harder to get to sleep. There were times when I would go for two or three days on a total of seven hours' sleep. If I continued, I knew that my health would suffer seriously.

At this point, just when desperation was creeping in, my Voice told me what was to happen next. My Voice can come at any time, but on this occasion I was meditating. The word 'meditation' covers a variety of mental activities. I go into a meditative state when I am healing – and sometimes when hoovering! I always make space during the day for meditation, even if it is only a short time; it is like going within myself to find a small space which, when entered, is infinite. (The nearest simile I can find is Dr Who's police box, the Tardis.) In this huge inner space, which has no barriers, I enter an area of Mind where everything is in a state of unrealised potential. It is then up to me to bring the potential into being, and to use it. It is often when I am in this area of potential that my Voice comes, sometimes with very clear verbal messages, sometimes as a more meditative feeling.

This was one of the times when the Voice gave me very clear instructions and a totally new and unexpected sense of direction. It told me, in the nicest possible way, that I was now required to go to university. Furthermore, although my personal preference would have been to study an arts-related subject, it quite clearly indicated that I must go for a science degree.

I immediately wanted to know: 'How? Why? When?' The Voice told me that I would be shown how, but why and when were not answered at the time.

I felt confused. I was still in the middle of Ivy's training – how on earth would I manage? I decided that if I had to study science I would choose biology and zoology, the scientific subjects I had enjoyed most at school. But how was I to set about it? I had acquired three O-levels at evening classes, but the prospect of slogging through the A-levels necessary for university entrance was daunting. For a scientific degree course I would probably need maths, my worse school subject. I was almost in despair.

As so often happens, my next step was made clear through an apparent coincidence. Other people keep cats and dogs, but I have always been fascinated by reptiles, and at the time I had some small lizards as pets. In Balham, in South London where Chris and I were living, there was a shop which sold and advised on reptiles. One day I was looking at their stock when I got into conversation with a girl who told me she was giving up work to go to university. She had information about Access Courses, a system which enables mature students without A-levels to qualify for university entrance after a year's study.

I had been told I would be shown, and here I was being shown. I promptly went for an interview with the Access Course organisers, and was accepted. I applied for a grant, and rather to my surprise was given one. But even with the grant, I couldn't have embarked on the course without Chris's support. She said, 'If you want to go to university, don't worry about money. We'll manage.'

By now I had learnt that when my Voice told me to do something, I should act on it. With extraordinary speed my whole life changed. In the autumn of 1987, six weeks after being told about my new direction, I had left my job and started a year's full-time Access Course.

During that year I had a thoroughly wonderful time: it was like being back at school, but much more fun. The college was at an adult education institute run by the now defunct Greater London Council, who were funding me. I studied food biology, the nearest I could get to pure biology that would be acceptable for university entrance. The course including microbiology, chemistry and food science and covered practical as well as theoretical work. Some of the students were going into catering science, so as well as the science subjects I studied nutrition and cookery.

London University had offered me a place provided I passed the Access course. Without studying very hard I gained enough knowledge to qualify. Only maths was a struggle: logical progressions have never been my forte. I couldn't believe it when I passed – I think I was given the answers intuitively. In September 1988 I started at London University.

This whole period was like the final part of a shamanic journey. I can see my life now as akin to an initiation taking place over a long, long time. My rebirth at five was simply the start. I had to gain experience of life and go through emotional learnings. Then there was the musical side, the harmonising. I had embarked on music for pleasure, and sound was to become important in my work. All this life training was woven into whatever else I was doing, a lot of it concurrently.

My first year at university was very joyful, although I didn't socialise much. My fellow students were all eighteen; I liked them, but I didn't go to discos or share their kind of lifestyle. All my life was outside, including our singing classes as well as studying with Ivy. I was a very busy person, but very happy. I was still puzzled as to how going to university could lead to my future in spiritual healing and teaching. When I asked my Voice, the only answer I got was: 'It's part of the programme – you just have to be patient.'

I was still living with Chris, very happily – or so I thought. In fact, at this time cracks were beginning to develop in our relationship, though I was too absorbed to take notice of them. I was beginning to realise what I had always sensed was my destiny. I felt as if I was emerging from a dark wilderness, and I was having to learn to deal with a new way of being.

During this transition, Chris's support of me was absolute and unselfish. But I was totally taken up with my own inner life and development, to the detriment of my emotional responsibilities. I genuinely loved Chris, but I took it for granted that she would meet my needs even though I was not giving her the time and space she needed and deserved. It must have been quite an ordeal for her, and I accept responsibility for my part in it.

For my second year at university I had chosen to specialise in zoology and ecology. This meant going through a first year of general biology, basically repeating the Access Course, including statistics and chemistry, at a slightly more advanced level. I cruised through it all rather coolly. I didn't work hard, and I didn't worry about it. I felt, 'Obviously all this training hasn't been anything to do with spiritual work, though I'm going to do that some time. They must want me to be an ecologist.' In the event I passed the first year exams reasonably well, except for statistics which I only scraped through.

I was still in my first year when I was led, as usual without realising it, in the direction planned for me. I had been recommended to go to a lecture on ecology by Dr Elizabeth Bergwyn, a biochemist at a major scientific research establishment. I mentioned this to my friends in Ivy's class. One of them turned out to be a researcher at the same centre; she said, 'Oh, I know Elizabeth – you ought to meet her. Mention my name to her.'

Dr Bergwyn was a dynamic lady in her forties; her lecture was on the importance of preserving the rainforests, which supply the planet not only with oxygen but with all kinds of medicines from wild plants. Afterwards I introduced myself and Dr Bergwyn invited me to her lab for a coffee. We chatted for a while about her lecture; then she said, 'Let's forget all this scientific stuff, and talk about psychic things.'

She turned out to be a closet psychic – an excellent healer and dowser, who dowses flower and homoeopathic remedies very accurately and effectively. Elizabeth Bergwyn, incidentally, is not the name she uses as a professional scientist, since she prefers to keep her scientific and healing activities quite separate.

We had a number of subsequent conversations and got to know each other quite well. One day Elizabeth said, 'I'd like to send a friend to you for some clairvoyant guidance.' Dr Tony Scofield turned out to be a cheerful, very alert-minded man in his forties. After his sitting he told me he was a lecturer in animal physiology at London University. Although most of his research work had been on the effects of natural compounds on enzymes he was also a dowser, and clearly took a positive interest in the paranormal and in healing energy. At that first meeting we began talking, albeit not very seriously, about the possibility of setting up some research. After that we met again several times and became good friends.

During my first university year my Voice brought through another very clear message: it told me I would graduate from Ivy's training. I was elated, not only because I would be receiving Ivy's rarely bestowed certificate but more importantly because, as my Voice explained, this meant that my real work could begin. The human mind being what it is, I was hard put to it to sit on my impatience while I waited for Ivy to tell me what I already knew.

This wasn't for another three months; Ivy didn't believe in telling people in advance, in case they should start thinking they knew it all before completing the training. Graduation from Ivy's training was far from automatic; she selected only those students whom she considered to have reached the required standard. In some years nobody graduated. Mine was a vintage year: there were four of us.

I had heard from former students that the graduation ceremony was a wonderful day when they realised they had made a promise to 'serve Spirit'. For me, it meant freedom. I owe Ivy a great debt; I respect her as a teacher and her training was fascinating and rewarding. Without it, I wouldn't have gained an understanding of the spiritualist movement and its view of clairvoyance. Ivy's teaching, as all good teaching should, provided me with a springboard from which to move on. But I find it very hard to follow anyone's teachings without question. My true allegiance was and is to my Voice, and throughout those three years I had followed its instructions not to talk about any of my direct knowledge. Consequently I had felt locked away, imprisoned by a set of philosophical structures which it was necessary for me to learn but which prevented me from expanding in all the areas I could feel bubbling around and within me. The graduation day was a release; I felt freed of a burden.

I had grown very fond of the people I graduated with; we had been through a lot of exciting learning together, and we continued to meet for a while as a group. But I knew on that day that I was about to move off in a very different direction, that I was at the beginning of something important. Significantly, one of the friends who came to the ceremony was Tony Scofield.

7

Science
Steps In

For some time Tony Scofield and I had been having a series of conversations, during which the idea of research developed from something it would be nice to do some time into a definite: 'Yes, let's do it!'

At this point, everything became clear to me. 'This is why I had to study science – nothing to do with being an ecologist or zoologist! All that bloody hard work, all those statistics and maths and chemistry, was purely so I would end up meeting people who would do some research with me!'

My thought process continued: if I was sent to university in order to do research, it must be to prove to the scientific community that healing energy was a fact, that 'impossible' things could and did happen. Obviously this was my role in life – to get the proof and convince the sceptics. Then I could retire gracefully and carry on quietly with healing.

Tony and I had several discussions before deciding what to do and how to do it. We had to design an experiment that would show healing energy as an objective reality, not just a placebo, a psychological effect. We had to think of a way of making something sick better, under laboratory conditions which could be repeated, and which could be written up and, we hoped, published in a scientific journal. There were a number of criteria.

Firstly, the experiment had to be non-psychologically influenced, which ruled out people as subjects. Secondly, the disease to be healed – whoever or whatever had it – must be artificially induced and therefore controllable, as opposed to healing someone already sick who might get better anyway. That also ruled out people. Some successful research had been carried out in the 1960s by a Canadian scientist, Dr Bernard Grad, who had shown the effects of healing on wounded mice. But neither Tony nor I was prepared to experiment with animals.

It was Tony who came up with the idea of cress seeds; they are alive, but as far as is known they don't have minds and are not susceptible to suggestion. Moreover, Tony thought it would be possible to induce some kind of disease in them artificially, and he set about finding a method of poisoning them without actually killing them. I was to give healing to the poisoned seeds, and we would see whether this affected their recovery time.

I visited Tony's flat in Folkestone once or twice while we worked out exactly how to set up the experiment; the pilot trials took place in his kitchen. He tried using various agents which would stress the seeds so that they would be sufficiently damaged to delay growth, but still able to recover and germinate. In the end he discovered that the best medium was, in scientific terms, a half-saturated solution of salt.

A saturated solution is one in which so many crystals are added to water that it will hold no more and they will not dissolve; seeds placed in a saturated solution are killed. A half-saturated solution consists of half that amount of crystals. Healthy seeds germinate in two to four days. Seeds soaked in a half-saturated solution of salt germinate after seven or eight days, and even then are not always as healthy as unstressed seeds. It was a good model, because so long as the solution remained the same, so did the effect: delayed germination and slightly unhealthy seeds.

The next step was for me to give healing to seeds that had been soaked overnight in this solution, to see whether the germination time would change. A few days after our two quick try-outs in his kitchen, Tony met me in London. He was tremendously excited. The seeds that had been given healing had germinated at double the rate of unhealed seeds. Now, he told me, we could start doing the experiment properly in his laboratory – though he added, 'Of course it won't work!'

This is how Tony recalls it:

I'll never forget coming up to London to see Geoff with the results of the first two experiments. Those first, early results were the most dramatic of all, because we had so many seeds piled together in a petri dish [a dish used to grow cultures in scientific laboratories]. Later, when we got into the lab, we spread them out as they had to be counted out by hand. But to start with, we just had a great lump of tiny seedlings.

When I found the results were positive, I must confess I wasn't altogether pleased! Because if you are suddenly faced with what I consider to be proof that seed-healing really does work, you're presented with an awful dilemma, and you've got to make a decision. Either you ignore it, and pretend it never happened, or you have to accept it. And once you accept it, your whole life changes. That's not easy; that's when things get difficult in many ways. But I had to accept it was real, and accept the consequences.

I was lucky to meet a scientist who would accept the consequences. The history of paranormal research is appalling. Most experiments that have worked once fail to work when they're set up again; that, I believe, is to do with the negative attitudes of sceptics, which create negative thought-forms.

Along with many people today, I believe that all thought is energy, just as everything that we are and observe is energy. Energy takes form, which means that all thoughts have a form of their own. What are often referred to in the healing world as thought-forms have a life of their own and, very importantly, a powerful influence of their own.

Scientific observers of experiments often have very rigid preconceptions about what is possible; the negative thought-forms they put out can create an almost solid barrier, which is bound to affect the outcome and makes working very difficult for the subject if he or she happens to be a psychic dealing with the delicate area of subtle energies (those energies on which healers and psychics draw, which appear to have an effect but at this stage lack scientific confirmation). Under these circumstances you need more than faith. Despite this, a great deal of successful research has been carried out under proper laboratory conditions, with irrefutable results, only to be totally disregarded by the scientific community. (See, for example, Dr Daniel J. Benor's *Healing Research: Holistic Energy Medicine and Spirituality*, Helix Verlag GmbH, Germany, September 1992. Dr

Benor has stated that out of 136 controlled experiments since 1952, 56 significantly demonstrate that healing has a positive effect. As he points out, if what was being tested was a pharmaceutical drug, that evidence would be enough for it to be accepted.)

Already during my degree course I had learnt a lot about the scientific mentality, and I had concluded that far from being an objective, fact-gathering discipline, science is actually a belief system, and a very sensitive belief system at that. For all its benefits – and I do not discount its benefits – science incorporates attitudes that are almost theological. When we came to do the experiments formally, the reactions from some quarters were really quite surprising. I learned a lot about scientific methodology, and how science approaches research into the psychic. Very often the response to strong evidence is: 'It can't exist because it breaks all the rules.'

Tony's open-minded attitude was in total contrast with others I had come up against. For instance, not long previously I had had a discussion about psychic phenomena and the paranormal with a professor of philosophy of science. He told me, 'Even if what you're saying is true, it's irrelevant! If the model we are using seems to work most of the time, that's all that matters.' To me, that is not logical. Anything that challenges the established scientific view of the world must have a relevance, yet many scientists seem unable to face up to such challenges, thus denying us the opportunity of a better understanding of the nature of our universe. For example, in a recent television programme the fact emerged that some people get Aids without being HIV-positive. A doctor commented that this was so rare as to be irrelevant, but I have a feeling that it may be more relevant than people think. If even a few people are getting Aids without the HIV virus, something is at fault in current beliefs about Aids.

With Tony's support and the prospect, I hoped, of providing incontrovertible proof of the effects of healing energy, I was beginning to get the bit between my teeth. Already in my life I had been the target of disbelief and criticism. At the start of the experiments proper, my attitude was: 'I'm going to show you that this can be done – I'm going to prove it.' I knew that was very naive, but I was inspired with a dogged, almost angry determination to make it work.

While we were planning the laboratory experiments, one or two other interesting things happened. Tony recalls an incident when I was visiting him at Folkestone:

> I was walking along the beach with Geoff one day, and he was getting above himself as usual – he is really keen and gets carried away by things; when his enthusiasm takes over one tends to be a bit left out. I like Geoff a lot, but because of that I take the mickey when he's around.
>
> Anyway, I picked up a plastic fork someone had dropped on the beach and said, 'All right, smart-arse, bend that!'
>
> And he bent it. It would have been impossible to bend in the normal way; it was so brittle it would have just snapped. He did it in front of me – it wasn't even warm. After he'd bent it, the ridges on the side hadn't even deformed – it was quite remarkable. I've kept it; any time I have doubts I look at that fork.'

I did several other experiments with Tony and his colleague David Hodges, some of them quite interesting and impressive, but never under strictly controlled laboratory conditions. On one occasion I altered the trace on an oscilloscope, which can be used to show changes in electromagnetic energy. They tuned it so that it would pick up 50 Hertz waves; then Tony asked me to concentrate on changing the visible wave with my hand near the aerial. Just by thought I was able to make the 50 Hz wave flatten and disappear; when I stopped, it reappeared.

Some people would say that this proves that my energy is electromagnetic, but as Tony comments:

> The fact that Geoff has an effect on another organism or another body means by definition that there must be a transfer of energy. But it doesn't mean it's got to be electromagnetic. Taking all the phenomena into account, including the cress seeds and fork bending, there is really no common factor that could involve electromagnetic radiation. The energy Geoff draws on simply isn't one that we comprehend at the moment.

Once we were clear about how we were going to conduct the experiments, Tony set up a proper protocol and brought in his colleague David Hodges, who was to measure the growth of the seeds. We used Tony's own laboratory at Wye College in Kent, going in on Sundays when there were no students around. Tony's son, who was studying to be an osteopath, came in to take notes. When we started, the Principal knew nothing about our activities: we used to creep in very secretly, with a cover story that Tony was doing overtime. Nobody except David Hodges and the lab assistant knew what was going on.

One great advantage of this particular experiment,

which we hope will be repeated by other people, is that it is not only simple but extraordinarily cheap! Briefly, I held about two hundred pre-poisoned seeds for three minutes and gave them healing; then I held a similar quantity of poisoned seeds without healing them. One hundred and twenty of each were then counted as they were put into petri dishes on wet filter paper.

Since David was to measure the results, he had to stay out of the lab while I was doing the healing. Tony's son coded the dishes, putting a note of the codes in a sealed envelope, and the seeds were then put in a growth room. Every day for the next five or six days David Hodges came in to measure how much the seeds had grown. They had to be carefully counted each time; it was a very plodding task. Only then were the codes broken so that he could assess the differences in growth between the healed and the unhealed seeds. We repeated this experiment six times in all.

Doing the actual experiments and repeating them in the lab gave me the confidence to show other people what I could do. This included fork bending, which I had actually started doing before the research, thinking it might be a good way of demonstrating what is possible with energy. However, it was only when I started that I realised it wasn't the best way for me. Even when it's genuine, it still looks like the sort of conjuring trick that is easily faked for television 'magic' shows. It is also still very much associated with Uri Geller, whom many people have tried to expose as a fraud – though in my opinion this is not the case.

Moreover, when the word got around, I started being asked to dinner parties and expected to destroy the cutlery. After a time I gave up accepting these invitations. I was not receiving direct guidance from my Voice at that time, and to some extent my ego had taken over. Nevertheless, I was aware that energy can be spiritual, and that bending forks was not the best way to demonstrate it.

However, before we had completed the experiments I gathered together a small group of friends at the offices of the Koestler Foundation in London. The Koestler foundation was set up to explore the paranormal which had interested Koestler in his latter years. They included Elizabeth Bergwyn and Ruth West, Director of the Koestler Foundation and a writer and researcher of the paranormal. Some of those who came had been with me on Ivy's course; having always kept to my instructions not to tell them what I could do, I now felt pleased to share my gifts with them.

I did some fairly basic experiments, including some metal bending. I also demonstrated that I could increase electromagnetic energy by getting compass needles to move: I do this by sitting close to them and thinking them into moving away from the north-south polarity.

Then for the first time I tried a different type of experiment with cress seeds. I don't know what prompted this; Tony told me later that in researching historical references he had come across an old book which stated that one of the ways in which shamans used to demonstrate their power was to germinate seeds.

I took along an unopened packet of cress seeds, only opening them in the presence of the group and under Dr Bergwyn's scientific eagle eye. I decided to add some water to them for a couple of minutes. Then I held the wet seeds in my hands and concentrated on giving them healing energy. Within three minutes around 30 per cent had started to germinate, with tiny but visible roots and some rudimentary leaves – the latter were a yellowish white as they had not had time to develop any chlorophyl. After that I tried the same experiment in the lab a couple of times, and managed in five minutes to get stalks with leaves on them; normally they would have taken twenty-four to thirty-six hours to grow.

Very soon after this we had the results of the experiments. They were phenomenal. In five cases out of six the rate of germination and growth of the healed seeds was at, or close to, double the rate of the unhealed seeds. Statistically, the recovery rates were so high against chance that in scientific terms there could be no doubt whatsoever that healing creates an effect. Tony and David subsequently wrote in a paper published in the *Journal of Alternative and Complementary Medicine* in September 1991:

'In mainstream scientific research odds of 1000:1 against a chance occurrence of the event being tested are considered to be highly significant and the hypothesis is considered proven. Most of our results showed odds of many millions to one against the differences being due to chance.' Tony has also commented: 'Geoff is particularly powerful, although I gather there are other healers who can do similar things. The beauty about Geoff's work was that he was prepared to come back over and over again. We repeated the experiment half a dozen times, which is very unusual.'

One interesting point is that, of the six experiments, the results of the first were only mildly significant. I put that down to my feeling unnerved the first time, because a laboratory creates such a difficult atmosphere. This is important when scientists work with psychics and healers; the environment and the atmosphere can contribute to success or failure. The people involved, both the subject and the observers, are part of the experiment. Thus it often happens that a pilot trial is set up quite casually; everyone feels comfortable and friendly, and the experiment works. The test conditions may not be totally adequate, but a sympathetic scientist will say: 'I accept this.' Then everyone gets excited and it is decided to repeat the trial under proper laboratory conditions. This time the poor psychic walks in and meets with a clinical atmosphere and negativity from the experimenters, who by now have convinced themselves that the experiment won't work. And it doesn't.

In our case Tony Scofield and David Hodges carried out the experiment rigorously in a proper laboratory, but they were not antagonistic; they were sympathetic in the sense of being relaxed and open-minded. They simply wanted to see what would happen, and there was no pressure on me either to succeed or to fail. That made a lot of difference. I also think a contributing factor was my own angry determination to prove it could be done.

When we saw the results we were all absolutely over the moon! Elizabeth Bergwyn was informed, and I told Chris and my family and friends; the next stage was to try to get the results published. The idea had been that if the series was successfully completed under proper conditions we would go to journals like *New Scientist* and say, 'Here is a scientific set of experiments which shows an effect of healing. Now publish that.'

Nobody did. The features editor of *New Scientist* had expressed an interest and was sent reports of the experiments as they were written up, but the then editor would not publish them. John Maddocks, the editor of *Nature*, was quoted in the *Daily Telegraph* of 25 April 1989 as saying that we were self-deluding, 'doing conjuring tricks without realising it'. Although not terribly surprised, I did feel very upset and angry: how could a man who had not even asked to see a report of the experiment make such a judgment? However, we didn't feel there would be anything to gain by replying.

Tony too met with some odd responses. He says:

I didn't expect anything else from *Nature*. A lot of
scientists will not believe, even if you present proof
to them on a plate, and it's not worth trying. But
I heard indirectly that people had commented on
our work, saying that the statistics were flawed,
all before we'd published anything or told anybody
about it. I couldn't believe it. They were making
judgments without even knowing what we'd done!

Some people wouldn't believe it if Geoff materialised an elephant in the middle of the Albert Hall.
The atmosphere is changing, but those people won't
change; they will die and lose their influence and
the younger people coming along will change things.
This is how changes occur, not by people changing
their minds.

Tony and David together wrote and submitted a paper
to the *Journal of the Society for Psychical Research* which
appeared nearly two years later in January 1991 (Vol.
57 pp. 321–43). Before acceptance, the paper had to be
sent to two independent anonymous referees in North
America for comment; both were obviously impressed
with it, and both recommended publication. A shortened
version appeared in the *Journal of Alternative Medicine* in
September 1991.

Tony and David thought long and hard before writing
the paper, and decided to bring into the open any points
that could be criticised; they included them in the Discussion (a formal part of all scientific papers in which
the results are analysed), which rather disarmed readers.
To this day, Tony tells me, they have received no serious
criticisms from anybody: 'So either nobody's interested,
or they can't see anything wrong with it. But again,

rumours have been put around. I've heard indirectly people muttering that we consider there are flaws in it. Neither David nor I have said any such thing.'

Meanwhile, the first piece of publicity to appear was an article in the *Daily Telegraph* on 24 April 1989. Elizabeth Bergwyn had mentioned our activities to an interested journalist, Sarah Stacey, who thought it sounded like a good story. She came to see us at Tony's lab, accompanied by a photographer, and did a very thorough interview. For their benefit I repeated the instant seed germination experiment I had done at the Koestler Foundation, and the photographer took pictures of seeds that had grown in my palm. Having arrived a sceptic, he left totally convinced.

The publication of Sarah's article initiated a change in public awareness of my work. To be featured in the *Telegraph* was itself quite an achievement; moreover, while quoting Maddocks' criticisms, Sarah introduced some more favourable comments by Professor David Bohm, Emeritus Professor of Physics at Birkbeck College.

Tony was not very keen on the work being publicised so soon. When the article came out he and David Hodges hardly dared go to work, fully expecting to be mocked and pilloried. In fact, they were pleasantly surprised by the general reception. Tony was particularly encouraged by the reactions of the new Principal of Wye College and the then Acting Head of Department, who commented: 'I keep an open mind about this. It's interesting, and I will support you, simply because I know from your previous track record that you're good scientists.'

'He was very positive about it,' Tony told me. 'He may not have believed it, but that didn't matter. On the basis of our track record, he was prepared as a good scientist to believe the experiments had been done properly and what we'd found was genuine.'

As a result of the *Telegraph* article, two TV crews came down to film us working in the lab. One of them was filming a programme for *Your Life in Their Hands*, but none of the material has ever been shown. None of us knows precisely why, but I suspect that it was partly because much of what happened occurred off-camera, which could have appeared to viewers like trickery.

Filming paranormal events is always difficult. Tony had already tried videotaping me while we did the experiment, but nothing would work on camera. Yet he had previously cast some seeds aside on a bench, and when he happened to glance out of the corner of his eye he actually saw one growing. When he looked at it fully, it stopped.

It is very difficult to work scientifically with camera crews around. We wanted to maintain the strictly controlled conditions – otherwise it would be easy for people to discredit the results. But the TV crew wanted something more visually dramatic; possibly hoping that I would produce an instant bunch of cress, they asked for us to work with lots of seeds.

Tony was very unhappy about this request. He explained that if we were to put a great handful of soaked seeds together in a dish they would go mouldy, which is precisely what happened. I had hoped they would still germinate after healing, and was very disappointed when they didn't. However, Tony was pleased in a way, since it proved his point.

Some odd things happened. The night before, as was his practice, Tony had put in a cupboard about a dozen beakers containing soaking seeds. Eight lots were soaking in the salt solution and four in plain water; all were covered with sealed plastic lids. At the beginning of the filming session he looked at the beakers before I started healing, and all was as usual.

During the filming, he went several times to the cupboard to take seeds out so that I could demonstrate healing them. Every time he took a beaker from the cupboard there would be a few growing cress plants inside; this happened with every beaker, including those containing the salt solution which should have delayed germination. Tony had to fish out the growing seeds before giving me the rest for healing. He kept apologising to the TV crew, explaining that this just shouldn't happen – it wasn't possible!

They said, 'Don't worry. We've worked with psychics and mediums before, and something like this always happens. It's uncontrollable.'

Tony has given this some thought and believes that the psychic energy I was generating instead of being directed at what he was trying to do, was going all over the place and affecting the seeds. He comments:

> At the end of the day, if you're going to believe in this, you've got to have an act of faith. I don't think anybody ever, is going to get 100 per cent cast-iron proof that this is genuine. You've got to take that little, maybe only tiny little step, that act of faith. Things were happening off camera – why not on camera?
>
> I don't think Geoff would agree with this, but it's almost as if some sort of intelligence is there, which is determined not to give the 100 per cent proof on film.

My own interpretation is that external intelligence and the inner mind are closely linked, and may have agreed at some level of consciousness that this was not the right time to have 'proof' of this kind.

Although the experiments did not make the sort of impact we might have liked, they did move us all forward. Tony concludes:

> The work Geoff did with us is so important because it was done under strictly controlled conditions. Of course the most important thing about Geoff is the fact that he helps people; that's all that really matters at the end of the day. But David Hodges and I would like to move on and spend more time doing healing research, based on strictly controlled lab work, even though it's a very difficult area.
>
> I would like to feel that the work we will do in the future, in a very modest way, will actually make people realise that perhaps healing is real – perhaps they can benefit from it if they take the trouble to try healing. If that's all it achieves I shall be happy. This is not an area one uses for career promotion – rather the reverse, in fact.
>
> Fortunately, in this country, one of the rights of university lecturers is the right to pursue, within the law, knowledge of an unpopular or controversial nature without risk of being persecuted or dismissed. This is a controversial area, but we are entitled to pursue it, whether people like it or not! Universities in this country are the last bastion of this kind of freedom.

For me, the experiments had two major results. Firstly, they began to place me in the public eye, giving my activities a respectable basis. The scientific community may ignore us, but television and radio interviewers do not; whenever I am interviewed, the scientific validation of my work is one of the hooks they can hang their questions on.

Secondly, it was a valuable learning process for me: was my purpose in being here to prove something to disbelievers, or was it to impart an energy of love and healing to other people? It became clear to me where my real values had to lie, and I have given up my stance of 'I'm going to show you!' The proof is there for those who are interested.

As Tony says, however impeccable the evidence, you cannot prove something to people who aren't ready to accept it. The whole venture has enabled me to see just how frightened people are when the mental structures they lean on begin to look uncertain. A major purpose for my being here is to show that not only are some of these structures imprisoning, but that in order for humanity to move forward they are going to have to break down. My work is not about converting people, or making them believe; the abilities I have been given are to help people who want to become self-responsible to open their mental doors to new perceptions.

The whole exercise has powerfully highlighted for me the importance of belief systems and structures. The approach you take to an experiment is an integral part of the results. If a scientist does an experiment which seems to prove a hypothesis, that does not mean that this result is an absolute, eternal truth. All it proves is that the hypothesis is true within the parameters of our present observation, and to say otherwise could be misleading.

The evidence for the objective existence of subtle energies is already well established, but if people do not want their mental structures changed they will not see it. You will hear scientists using arguments to denigrate research into the paranormal that they would not use in respect of any other scientific experiment. These attitudes are changing; there are scientists who are exploring the possibility that there is more than the mechanistic view. These are the ones working at the fringes of physics, like Paul Davies, Fritjof Capra, Rupert Sheldrake and the late David Bohm.

At least our experiments have added to the total body of successful research into the paranormal. As for the future of such research, of course scientists must set up proper controls to make sure they are not fooled. But if they are to get anywhere, they should start working with psychics in helpful surroundings, or within a healing context – not just in clinical laboratories. I regard the experiments as important for others who need to gain information through the scientific model. I leave them behind me in the hope that they will encourage others. I know my own way forward.

8

Manifestation

My involvement with the scientists was like the last
stepping stone on a long journey. Now my destination
was in sight. As my work has grown, my own role in
this has become increasingly clear: my link with Source
Energy is to help people towards our vital next step.
We are at a point in history which is the beginning of
major evolutionary change. This will affect not only the
spiritual development of human beings, but the future of
the planet and of the whole Vortex within which we are
contained.

There have been influxes of Source Energy throughout
history when society has been undergoing huge changes.
It was implanted in Christ and the Buddha, but also
in many, many others who have never achieved public
acclaim, both in the past and today. They include not
only healers and spiritual teachers but creative artists,
writers and composers, as well as political and social
leaders.

The influence of the Source here and now is part of

our current evolution. Numerous Source people and groups are working towards producing an awareness that will gradually make that evolution part of everyone's consciousness; although it will not be completed in this generation, what is happening now is the seeding of a different kind of human being.

As we are seeing, the planet is already undergoing important social, political, economic and ecological changes. Even more dramatic changes are imminent, and it is necessary for more and more people to understand both the nature of this evolution and the fact that they have an active part to play in it. It is my role, and that of others, to help spread this understanding.

Back in the spring of 1989, although I knew my work was to expand, I couldn't see how. It was the *Daily Telegraph* article that set things in motion. Two local papers followed it up, focussing on the healing aspect of my work, which spread my name more widely. Suddenly people in need of healing were making enquiries.

I gave up my degree course, which had served its purpose, and started giving healing and spiritual guidance fairly full-time from home. I was still very much at the beginning of my new road, and there were some false starts on the way. As a result of the *Telegraph* article I was approached by London Weekend Television, who invited me to appear in an early evening magazine programme. This experience taught me a number of lessons, the first being never to agree to appear on a programme I know nothing about. But I was extremely flattered to be asked, and accepted with alacrity.

The item in the programme was entitled 'Germinator'. Tony Scofield had also been invited to take part, and I naively expected it to be a serious representation of our experimental work. The programme opened with some filmed footage of me giving healing; the main part went out live from a school laboratory hired for the occasion. Tony brought along some unopened packets of cress seeds which I was to try to make germinate in two minutes.

It had not occurred to me to check out what kind of programme it was. It turned out to be the TV equivalent of the tabloid press. I went on quite unprepared for the rudeness of the producer and the other people involved. I believe now that they had decided beforehand to set me up in order to make the whole issue as controversial as possible.

To begin with, I was introduced with great scepticism. Then, as I was concentrating on giving energy to the seeds – which does need concentration and a supportive atmosphere – the presenter turned to the camera and said, 'Now we will see whether the experiment works, or whether Geoff is a fraud.' The suggestion was that the opposite of success is fraud. I succeeded in getting some seeds to germinate; even so, some of the people working on the programme were still disbelieving afterwards and openly rude to me. The general implication was that I had produced the germinating seeds by sleight of hand.

A few days later they told me that viewers had been phoning in to say I must have been cheating: would I like to come back next week and do it again? As there was no way I wanted to repeat the experience, I simply said I wouldn't be available the following week. I already had other commitments – for one thing, since the programme the phone had barely stopped ringing with requests for healing.

Many people would jump at the chance to get on television; I found it difficult to escape! Next day there was a long message on my answering machine suggesting that refusing to go back would prove I had been cheating.

I responded by sending a letter of complaint by courier to the Managing Director of LWT.

Next, a young woman researcher turned up on my doorstep, wearing the shortest skirt I have ever seen. She told me that a famous psychic had offered £5000 to me and £5000 to charity if I would go back and germinate seeds in front of him and one or two other experts like the magician David Berglas, and if they were satisfied that it was not a trick. I told her bluntly that they had misjudged the sort of person I was: I was not interested in psychic duels or reducing my work to the level of a circus act.

After this categorical refusal I was astonished to hear a commercial on LBC announcing my forthcoming appearance on next week's programme in the 'Psychic Challenge of the Year'. I wrote a furious letter to the Managing Director insisting that they withdraw the announcement. They continued to try to pressurise me into appearing, and I had to get a lawyer to write to them before the commercial was withdrawn.

The following week the programme was broadcast live from the same laboratory; Tony Scofield went again, and they also brought in the psychic who had issued the challenge, together with David Berglas. They announced that I had written to say that taking part in a challenge would demean my work, but 'We are waiting, Geoff, if you would like to come in.'

They finally acknowledged that I wasn't coming and the psychic said he didn't blame me. David Berglas tried to show how seeds could be made to appear to germinate instantly by the old conjurer's trick of palming; he used mustard seeds, which are bigger and easier to palm than cress, and Tony commented afterwards that everyone close to him could see what he was doing. As a conjurer Berglas was impressive, but even the presenter agreed after the broadcast that he could see him using sleight of hand, whereas – not surprisingly – he hadn't seen me do any such thing.

Around the same time I was invited to take part in a radio phone-in: this was a happier occasion, with some quite interesting results. You might think that making cress seeds germinate on radio would be a non-event, but a member of the public was invited to watch in the studio, and the presenter described the experiment. He told listeners that if he hadn't seen the seeds growing for himself he would never have believed it.

Before energising the seeds I asked listeners to attune to the energy, since some people might find things happening to them like cutlery bending or watches stopping. One woman telephoned to say that during the broadcast a cupboard full of crockery had wrenched itself off her kitchen wall, screws and all; another told us she had watched the plates in her kitchen rack jump up, turn round and land back in the rack without breaking. Similar things have happened on other broadcasting occasions. A certain proportion of listeners are receptive to the energy I send out, and this triggers their own psychic and psychokinetic abilities, albeit temporarily.

What happened next had been potentially possible all along, but could not manifest until I had made the mental decision to be a lot more careful about how I projected my work. I accepted an invitation to visit a spiritualist church in Swindon, whose organisers had read about the cress seed experiments in the *Psychic News*. I told them that I wouldn't germinate seeds for them, but would give some healing and see what happened. I still had no direct information from my Voice, but I knew beforehand that something major was about to occur.

At the Swindon church I invited four or five people to come up and sit in a row for healing; I often give healing to small groups together, since I can channel a lot of healing energy very rapidly. I asked them all to tell me what they were suffering from, so that I could relay this information (with their permission) to the assembled company. Then I walked up and down the row a couple of times, putting my hands over their heads.

As I did so, for the first time in public I allowed the full force of the Source Energy to manifest. I was immediately filled with a sense of elation, and a joyful relief that I was at last going to do real Source work in front of other people. At the same time I felt lifted up into the Source, experiencing the absolute knowledge that I was really connected with and tapping into something immense.

Although I knew that the Source was going to produce something extraordinary, I had not been told what it would be. Suddenly a mass of fine, scented powder started to fall from my hands. It was like vibhouti, the sacred ash that Sai Baba materialises from nowhere to give to his followers. The ash from my hands was more coloured than vibhouti; some of it was pale, some of it reddish brown, and it was highly aromatic. The whole hall was filled with its perfume.

The scented powder continued to pour out of my hands in huge quantities, showering my patients and pouring on to the floor. There was an awed silence from the audience, followed by an eruption of talk and a rush as people scrabbled to scoop up ash up from the floor.

I knew this marked the opening of another door. I was beginning to gain a much deeper realisation of my role. I knew that the ability to bring about physical materialisations of spiritual energy is a direct manifestation of the

Source, and I knew that these manifestations would now continue.

Within the week I was doing some healing when scented oil started to appear in my hands. At the same time my Voice told me that this was to be the main manifestation that I would produce, since it was a physical expression of healing energy which could be seen, smelt and also absorbed by the person I was healing. It also told me that this ability has always been a part of me, and that although I don't consciously remember it, I had produced oils in my hands when alone as a child. The gift was only released again when it became appropriate.

My gifts are rather like the pictures in an Advent calendar; they have been there all along, but concealed. Only at the right time can the windows be opened to reveal them. I believe the oil can materialise simply because a doorway has been opened that gives me access to all the dimensions of Mind.

Since then, materialising scented oil has become one of the main ways in which I bring spiritual energy into reality. Sometimes the oil pours from my hands, or coats a crystal if I am using one. The perfumes vary. Many are natural – floral, herbal or lemony, similar to the essential oils used in aromatherapy. A number are very difficult to put a name to; they seem to be mixtures, sometimes very odd ones, and there are some that nobody can recognise.

The oil I manifest is not an inert substance but a living, changing experience: when I am healing or teaching a group of people, the aroma usually changes as I go round the group, and I may end up having produced two, three, four or even six different aromas. The scent will also change while I am giving healing to a single person. This shows that the energy being given is adjusted to the needs of the individual. Now, with experience of the oils, I can relate the aroma to the kind of energy a particular person needs.

Not everyone receives oil from my hands every time I give healing; for example, when I was healing a group of twelve people recently only five or so were given oils. For the recipient, absorbing the oil is important since it carries a healing energy; equally important is the inner change that occurs when the oil appears. Some people find the experience extremely moving, and it helps them to make great emotional and spiritual shifts. This, I believe, is the purpose of the manifestation.

One of my present colleagues, Kath Christof, has had many experiences with the manifested oils. Still in her twenties, she came from America to England to study drama and acted for two years with a famous British theatre company. In September 1990 she found her way to a class I was running; this is how she first witnessed the oil manifesting:

There were about fifteen of us in the class; we sat in a circle and Geoff asked one of the students to go into the centre and hold a crystal. We all sniffed it beforehand, and it was an ordinary, odourless crystal. The person holding it sat in the centre with the crystal point down. Geoff was sitting about six feet away. Oil started appearing in his hands, and he focused on the crystal, asking all of us to focus on it too. The same oil that was on his hands started dripping off the crystal six feet away. It was an exercise to show how thought energy and healing energy can work at a distance; you don't have to have your hand over something for it to take effect. That was my introduction to Geoff's work!

121

You either take something like this on board or you don't. At the time I couldn't *not* believe it because it happened in front of me. But a part of your mind say 'It can't be! Unless I change every rational thought that I've ever had.' That's what I think a lot of Geoff's work forces people to do. You have to accept it because it happens in front of your eyes. Once you do, you have to recognise other things that challenge your whole belief system and its structure. That wasn't instant for me; but over a period of time I've found my whole belief structure changing as a result.

This is a major purpose of these manifestations. One patient of mine was an Irish nurse, a Roman Catholic. (I am, by the way, never concerned about the religious or other beliefs of patients when they come to me.) She worked in a holistic medical practice, where she used aromatherapy oils in massage. After a few healing sessions she was able to avoid an operation for her gynaecological problem. Later, she commented:

> I'm sure the healing had an effect on my spiritual life. The first time the oil came, I actually grabbed Geoff's hand, I thought, 'He's got something up his sleeve!' He hadn't. I asked a friend afterwards if she could smell the oils and she said yes, she could. I was glad, because I'd thought maybe I was just imagining it.
>
> When it happened again, I thought, 'Now I know Jesus did change water into wine! It is possible.' I hadn't believed things like that before.

Often the oils will manifest on a person some time after I have given them healing. Two days after having some healing from me Kath was walking down the street when she wiped her forehead and found oil on it; I have had several similar reports from other patients. Because Kath is particularly attuned to my work, I have been able to turn water into oil for her to use in aromatherapy. This is how she remembers it:

> For this particular batch, Geoff took a jug of tap water and poured some into a ceramic kitchen bowl. He put his hand in the bowl, and the water started turning to oil. He said to me, 'That's for you.'
>
> We left the room to make a cup of tea; when we came back the oil was spreading in the bowl. There was water on the bottom and oil on the top. We went away again and when we came back not only was there four times more oil so the bowl was filled with half water, half oil – this time the split was *vertical*, half water on one side and half oil on the other. The line was really distinct. It was very strange.
>
> I bottled the oil and use it in healing sessions. I just need one drop on my finger, and it spreads all over my hands, and keeps spreading and changing as I use it.

Shortly after I had begun manifesting oils a curious series of events showed me another lesson about the use of the power I had been given. They began when, in meditation, my Voice gave me a very clear warning that I was going to be presented with some choice which would be exceedingly dangerous.

Like everyone I had heard of the Russian monk Rasputin, famous as a healer, who had enormous influence over Tsar Nicholas II and his family and became involved with Russian politics. But I had never given him any particular thought until I found him being brought to my attention. First, I saw a film about him on television which I found intriguing, so I read a couple of books about him, one of them by Colin Wilson. Soon afterwards a patient gave me a rare book – an account of Rasputin's life, written shortly after his death by a Russian author. As I read these biographies, I found myself recognising the energy that worked in Rasputin, and I also realised that the many stories and rumours about his life are often inaccurate and conflicting. But what made the biggest impression on me was that the course of action he chose ultimately led to his assassination in 1916. Yet fascinating though all this was, I could see no particular reason at the time for my attention to be drawn to Rasputin until, soon afterwards, something happened that made it all clear.

When someone has the type of energy that I have, there will always be people who want to misuse it for other purposes, including political ones. One day a man came to me for healing who had been told about my ability to materialise healing oil. After two or three sessions, he announced that he was an agent for a Latin American government. Knowing how accurate a powerful psychic can be, he offered me a huge amount of money to act as a psychic informant and identify enemies of the state. This may sound far-fetched, but I have met my share of eccentrics and knew that, although this man was odd, his offer was genuine. In some countries psychic powers are widely respected and are exploited in this kind of way.

Despite the size of the sum on offer, it wasn't really a temptation. It was not only morally wrong; it would have put me in the position of a Rasputin. And, like him, had I chosen to take on any kind of political role I might not have survived very long. Rasputin had Source Energy, and his true purpose was to help to bring change to a very static, feudal society. Unfortunately, the human side of him led to his downfall. He had chosen to exploit his gifts by using power over others, and was murdered not because of his gift of healing but because of his influence over the Tsar and particularly the Tsarina.

I realised then that my mind had been resonating with Rasputin's mind through the link of Source Energy, in order to reinforce the warning I had received from my Voice. What we seemed to have in common was a very powerful drive for life which in my case I have to keep in check, because it could drag me away from my direction. Another parallel is a sense of invincibility, but whereas I experience this as a spiritual invincibility, Rasputin made the mistake of believing it was physical. Source Energy is very powerful but not omnipotent; those who have been granted it retain their free will and cannot be coerced into using it for good. So while some people use it to help our spiritual evolution, there have always been some who have been tempted to use it for personal power. I should add that when it is used for evil purposes, it ultimately backfires on the user.

Much more recently I was taken during meditation into the mind of Mozart. This experience was profoundly beautiful, although I became aware that aspects of Mozart's life were very difficult. I have always felt an affinity with his music; now I felt the actual process as he composed. It was unbelievable, almost painful, because the music would not stop coming: it poured through with no thought, almost like a painful rage. This was another aspect of the Source Energy, in the form of pure creativity. As with Rasputin, we shared the same Energy; I am not claiming to have been Mozart in a previous life.

Neither of these incidents should be confused with

reincarnation. Reincarnation has a reality of its own, although I believe its nature is misunderstood. For one thing, past lives are only 'past' because we live in time. If it were possible for someone to stand outside time, they would see several lives as different aspects of the same individual – living forms existing in parallel.

Secondly, I believe that reincarnation is a feature of the Vortex within which we live, rather than a universal spiritual law. Within the Vortex energy cannot disappear, therefore minds do not die, and reincarnation serves as a method of enabling them to continue. Ultimately, as we evolve towards our eternal spiritual nature, it will no longer be necessary.

After I had been working from home for two or three months I was invited by Brenda Marshall, then President of the College of Psychic Studies, to give regular healing and clairvoyant sittings at the College. The CPS already ran an evening healing clinic at which several healers saw patients on a first-come first-served basis. I believe I was the first full-time private healer they had ever employed, and I saw people by appointment for up to four days a week.

This gave me a much more regular life and a regular, if not enormous, income, a percentage of which went to the College. At last I was earning a living through my real vocation. I don't believe in charging huge amounts for healing; there are a few healers whose very high fees, in my view, give critics a stick to beat all healers with. At the same time, I am not one of those who believe it is wrong to charge anything for spiritual gifts. I trust my Voice and my intuition, which have told me that since this is my life's work I should not be afraid to support myself through healing.

Like many healers who get publicity I also found

myself acquiring fans. I had to keep aware of the nature of my work, and not allow my ego to get carried away by adulation. My healing work went well, and for the first few months I also gave clairvoyant sittings; this had been part of my training with Ivy, and I was expected to do it. However, I didn't see this as an important area of my work, and after a time I concentrated on healing alone. Of course, like any healer I would now and again receive guidance for people, and when appropriate I would pass it on to them.

As always happens with healing, some patients failed to respond; at other times some wonderful things happened. I remember in particular one week when coincidentally two babies were brought to me with brain tumours. Both were about eighteen months old, and both tumours were seriously advanced. One of them recovered after one healing session. His parents rang me a month or so later to tell me the tumour had disappeared. Sadly, the other baby died. Healing is never predictable.

There was also a woman who recovered from a back problem after I had found myself removing a piece of fibrous tissue from her back. Some people call this 'psychic surgery', a label I prefer not to use because of its associations with some practitioners who use instruments to practise invasive techniques, which I do not. For me, it is another form of materialisation: it is possible to dematerialise matter within a body and rematerialise it outside, and for this it is not necessary to open the body.

I do not see this as a more valuable or more powerful method of healing than any other; but for some people it is a way not only of removing something, but also of opening their minds. I do it very rarely and do not offer it as a regular treatment, but only when the time is right.

I spent 1989 steadily building up my experience both in the College and outside it. Unfortunately the increased security of my working life did nothing for my private life. Perhaps if I had shared my work with Chris, things would have been different. She was certainly not against what I was doing, although she wasn't sure about the importance of the psychic or the real purpose of my work. Possibly this came from her Buddhist ideas; Buddhists would say that manifestations such as I was producing are transitory phenomena on the spiritual path, which should not be regarded as important. This, of course, is not my view. At the same time, I made no real attempt to include Chris in my psychic activities, which increasingly took me out of the house and into other circles.

In every other way we had a deep, close and loving partnership. But as my work took more and more of me, Chris felt it reasonable that I should put some time and energy aside for the person I was sharing my life with. But I couldn't do it. I had a real fear that if I committed myself to her totally the work would suffer, though Chris assured me it wouldn't. I felt I would have to give her much more time, and would have to moderate what I did.

Chris's one big cry of complaint was that in the end I turned everything back to me and my needs, and not to what she needed. We began having a lot of arguments, which I usually won – not because Chris was wrong and I was right but, partly because of the energy I can tap, I have an amazing ability to argue. I could produce elaborate constructions to turn her statements into an attack on me, when in actual fact she was asking for something quite simple, such as a little space and time and for me to think of other things including her emotional welfare.

What I finally and painfully learned during this

process was to see what I am like, and to be open and honest about it. Chris held up a mirror in which I could see how very self-centred and driven I was, and how difficult that makes it for anyone else to get a look in. At the time, I could see that there was another point of view, that she had other needs which were valid. But I wasn't able to fulfil them.

There may appear to be a dichotomy here: I was a healer, and healing is an expression of love, albeit a totally compassionate, unemotional form of love. Yet many healers have problems in their private lives. I no longer believe it is possible at the same time to do healing work and to behave uncaringly towards the person closest to one, but it has taken me a long time to get that balance right.

At the level of Source Energy, love is part of the creative force of Infinite Mind, and at that level it is not emotional. In our human existence, love is a very special part of the creative need to explore and understand each other; it is important because we would do nothing if we didn't have the need to explore and love and express ourselves. But within this dimension our emotions, however powerful, are limited and often unclear.

At the time, I made being busy an excuse to avoid facing the issue. I was so steeped in my work and my sense of vocation that I was hardly ever at home. After a day at the College I would go on in the evening to visit patients or give demonstrations and talks. I was still somewhat dazzled by the media attention I had received, and would go and lecture to almost anyone who asked me to. This included public demonstrations of my work which I gave as part of the College programme. My energy could still affect magnetic fields, electric lights and electrical gadgets like tape recorders, although it was more controlled than in my childhood. I still sometimes demonstrated fork bending.

I did not regard such phenomena as important; rather they seemed a side-effect of the energy that my body was using and developing. But I was still hoping to get across to people the idea that there are levels of energy which cannot be seen, and which can affect the material world. But when somebody stands on a stage making impossible things happen it is difficult for the audience to see this as a spiritual activity; there are always overtones of magic acts. I have now come to the conclusion that some of them actually detract from my real aims.

My time at the College was valuable to my own development. Seeing patients day after day, and learning to deal with all kinds of people, was a wonderfully interesting experience; it taught me how to trust my intuition to say the right things at the right time and – equally importantly – when not to speak at all.

9

'William'?

In November 1989, on the instructions of my Voice, I formed a small group of people who were keen to work with me and with whom I knew I could work. Our aim was to explore the energies that I was tapping into: in particular, how to transform spiritual energies into physical reality. Equally importantly, the group would provide me with the opportunity to bring into the open the knowledge that was latent within me. I started it with a sense of excitement.

Brenda Marshall, President of the College of Psychic Studies, was very enthusiastic about the idea, and offered us the use of a college room on Monday evenings. The regular members were friends I had made during Ivy's training, two of them with the same Source Energy as myself.

As I have already mentioned, Source Energy has been implanted in a number of people on this planet today, whom I have come to call 'Source people'. It is implanted at a time of critical illness or accident, but is not always immediately activated as it was in my own case. It can lie dormant in potential Source people, and may be 'switched on' so that they can be called to service at a particular time of need. All the Source people I have been in contact with have been naturally drawn to me, and when I have spoken to them about Source Energy they have immediately known what I was talking about even though they might not use the same terminology. Something similar is happening to other Source people in groups all over the world.

Source people are given the option to join in Source work, but no pressure is put on them and they have the free will to choose whether to use the energy and also how to use it. So another important purpose of the group was to allow the Source people among us to choose freely whether they wished to become part of the future Source work. During the next couple of years one or two people with Source Energy were introduced to the group and worked well with us for a while, but finally decided that this path was not right for them and exercised their freedom of choice to move off in different directions. The change in their own perceptions resulting from the group work would ultimately have an effect on all the people they would meet in their individual work and lives.

At the start the group included Ivy's former second-in-command Roger Stone; a good friend of mine, he taught clairvoyance on Ivy's course while working in 'real life' as a civil servant. Brought up in a Salvation Army family, and trained in spiritualist teachings, he had to work hard to expand out of his early conditioning. Roger was one of those with Source Energy, though he did not realise it until it was pointed out to him during the group sessions. He has a nice combination of psychic gifts with a logical, carefully thinking mind. He joined us with his wife Rosemary, also a clairvoyant, a strong, quiet and reserved person possessed of great inner wisdom.

Our third member, Trudy Brown, was a highly experienced medium who had worked with Ivy for many years. She is a very refreshing character, dependable and down to earth, who always speaks her mind honestly. I admired the courage with which she took on new ideas after many years of working as a traditional medium.

In January 1990 the group was completed by another Source person, Karen Harley. A business manager in her late twenties, she had joined Ivy's course after me. When I first met her in 1987 she struck me as intelligent and attractive, but what instantly drew my attention to her was her energy. It was the first time in my life that I had recognised an active Source Energy in another person. I didn't comment on it at the time, but later she told me that she had had a near-death experience as a child when she was concussed by a fall. For a few seconds her physical life had been in the balance, enabling the Source Energy to come in, although less dramatically than in my case. Karen and I understood each other well and became good friends.

The group met weekly at the College throughout 1990. I had been told that we should work to understand the mechanisms of energy, which are often erroneously explained in terms of spirits, the view favoured by most of the psychics who worked at the College. Although the phenomena we produced were akin to those well documented in spiritualism, our approach had nothing in common with traditional spiritualist seances. There was no atmosphere of hushed reverence, no prayers or requests for visitations. Rituals were unnecessary. My Voice had a say in what happened, but it was in no way a 'spirit guide'. I was beginning to understand that it was

in fact a part of me, thought it was not yet the right time
to declare it.

From January we kept detailed records, noting down
events and tape-recording our questions and comments.
They now fill a large ring binder and we hope to publish
a fuller version of its contents separately, together with
more recently channelled material.

We started by looking at purely physical phenomena.
Our first project was to get a table to move by itself –
which we did, from the second evening. Spiritualists,
who have experimented with 'table-turning' since the
last century, have tended to explain self-motivated tables
as being influenced by spirits, while some people regard
such experiments as evil. There is no logical reason for
this. As a group we were learning to deal with our
mind energy, and how to combine our different minds
to work together. Spirits or other entities have nothing
to do with mind energy, or psychokinesis (PK). And
there is nothing inherently 'evil' about mind: it is the
use of mind that makes it either good or evil. A number
of successful experiments in table-tilting and levitation
have already been carried out through the use of mental
energy or psychokinesis without resort to spirits. Guy
Lyon Playfair gives some good descriptions in Chapters
9 and 10 of his book *If This Be Magic* (Jonathan Cape,
London, 1985).

We always prepared the room in the same way, with
a blanket over the window, the smoke detector light
covered, all the doors locked to prevent interruptions,
and all white light turned off. In the background we
played music tapes quietly – usually modern jazz – for
our own pleasure rather than for any esoteric purposes.

Some people have criticised the fact that we started
out in total darkness, since this could lay us open to

accusations of cheating. Cheating would, of course, have been pointless; we were not trying to prove anything but simply seeking to gain information, in as relaxed a way as possible. The reason we kept the lights out, or low, particularly during the early sessions, was that even in my paranormally trained group one or two people had a psychological problem in suspending their disbelief. Sitting in darkness and cutting out visual input helps to overcome the logical conditioning which makes people believe 'this can't happen', thus actually preventing unusual things from happening. At the start it was easier to get the table moving when we couldn't watch it.

There were four of us present the first time the table moved. In the near-darkness Trudy, Roger, Rosemary and myself sat at a round table, two feet in diameter, our fingers lightly resting on its surface. I said, 'Let's assume that when the energy is right the table will start to move.' Then we just chatted, gossiped and told each other jokes as if it were an ordinary social occasion. I was convinced that conscious effort wasn't necessary. If we simply put the thought out, our minds would produce the results.

We were putting no pressure on the table, but before long we felt it tremble and quiver; then, at our request, it tilted towards each of us in turn. Next it began a gentle rocking from leg to leg, which lasted about a minute. Once we had turned off a distracting light shining under the door, the table became very lively. It tilted on two legs past the point of balance, and remained tilted when we took our hands off it. When we replaced our hands it pirouetted round the room, moving from one leg to another in a slightly drunken fashion; we had to follow it around to maintain contact. In the early days it sometimes tilted so far that it toppled on to the floor, but after a time it would tilt past the point of balance without falling.

Eventually its movements became more controlled, and it began to hop in the air. By week seven, at Roger's suggestion, we used a blue, 15-watt light bulb, providing our first artificial light. That evening the table started levitating, rising straight into the air several times to about five feet. When we asked it to go higher it levitated to over six feet, and we had to stretch up our arms to keep touching it. There it stayed for about a minute.

This was a momentous occasion, when the perception of all the group's members was immediately changed. Trudy was particularly astonished; she had experienced table-tilting before in her spiritualist career, but never table levitation. I had had no doubts about the extent of the energy available; for me this was not so much a confirmation of its power, but the beginning of sharing that energy with other people. The whole event forged stronger links between us as a group.

Later we managed to produce similar performances with the lights on; we even managed to video a small table moving. We also experimented with a larger table, though we mostly used the smaller one. Larger tables are not harder to move, but there is a psychological factor: when people see a large table, they doubt whether their minds can move it and this doubt affects the outcome.

The table continued to be active during most of our meetings that year. Its rocking at the start became our signal that the energy was flowing. From quite early in our experiments we began hearing raps from underneath it which we could use to give us 'yes' and 'no' answers to questions. It would also bid us 'goodnight' at the end of an evening, often by doing a little jig or tilting, as if bowing, towards each of us in turn.

Any spiritualist witnessing the table's behaviour could be forgiven for believing that it was activated by some kind of spirit or conscious entity. In fact, all we were doing was allowing our own energies, which are a part of our consciousness, to become sufficiently external to move the table. Its playful character simply reflected our own relaxed approach.

These kinds of phenomena are produced when psychic energy is intelligently directed by the thoughts, will and beliefs of those present so that it can manifest in a way that affects the material world. In terms of physics, there is enough energy in a square metre of air to lift a very heavy table. What happens is that energy is removed from the air around or above the table, which becomes quite cold, and transferred to beneath the table, which becomes quite warm. It is not the hot air that lifts the table, but the release of molecular energy.

In terms of the potential of Source Energy, these phenomena were relatively minor. I have a very strong energy which helped us to get immediate results, but I think that any group of people with the right attitude, who are dedicated enough to sit with their hands on a table every week for several months, would succeed in getting it to move. This task does not require a high level of spirituality, but it is simply a way of using mental energy – though anyone who believes that it could be harmful should obviously not attempt it.

The experiments were actually a means to an end. As the group's perceptions changed and the barriers of doubt came down, more of their energy was released into the group to be used in further exploration.

On 5 February that year we started receiving written messages. That evening I was prompted to place a pad and a small pencil in the centre of the table, and to ask for some writing. We turned out the lights, keeping a torch handy so that we could inspect progress; then we placed our hands on the table and asked for it to rap when things were ready. After one rap, we switched on the torch and saw that the pencil had been moved and a small mark had appeared on the paper. We heard the pencil drop to the floor, but when we looked it had completely disappeared.

We turned the light out again and, while we were still wondering where the pencil had gone, we heard it scratching on the paper. At first, all that appeared was a series of unintelligible letters but, like the table, the pencil seemed to 'learn' and was soon giving us sensible answers to questions. It never used punctuation, incidentally, so for the sake of clarity we have added punctuation in the extracts that follow.

We asked who was communicating with us: 'William', the pencil wrote, followed by the names of each group member; this indicated that the energy involved was a part of our shared mind. The handwriting, childlike at first, rapidly improved. At the end of the evening William told us in writing when to finish, and signed off: 'I love you.'

There was still no question of our communicating with a spirit. Later on, the writing explained to us that we had been given the name 'William' because, at that stage, the mental conditioning of the group was such that we needed or expected to be communicating with an individual personality. But this identity was purely a mental construct, not a real person. Readers may be familiar with the Philip experiment conducted in Toronto in the 1970s by a group led by Professor George Owen. They invented a 'ghost' called Philip, complete with fictional biography, with whom they became able to communicate as though he were an actual individual (see I. Owen and M. Sparrow, *Conjuring Up Philip*, Fitzhenry & Whiteside, Ontario 1976). We had not set out deliberately to create William but, like Philip, he was at least in part the product of our group mind. He was also more than that.

Messages from William became a regular feature of our meetings. Once we used a luminous board to give us minimal lighting, and were able to witness the extraordinary sight of the pencil in action, walking up and down the paper on its own, surprisingly fast.

From time to time we would question William's identity; each time the answer was more profound. On 4 June, asked whether it was William who was writing, the pen commented: 'Stop labelling. We are all the same. We, like you, are only individual in our thoughts [in order] to differentiate. All things are just energy in which patterns may be shown and then disappear. William is only a name, it is not an individual.' In September, asked to tell us more about who was writing, William identified 'himself' quite directly with the Source. The pen wrote: 'I am the personification of the intelligence that has always been. I have no identity except when you observe, but it is needed for our communication.' When I asked what 'intelligence' meant in this context, the writing continued: 'Intelligence is an innate part of your universe. Because you are at the moment in an individual observance [i.e. seeing events from an individual viewpoint] it is hard to think of mind without individuality. You are from the Source and you are therefore not just an ego; but to communicate, the energy appears as an individual.'

The words 'observation' and 'observance' featured frequently in William's communications, and later in our verbal channelling, and they are important. They refer, basically, to what we see from where we are at this moment, including our inner state, our beliefs, prejudices and expectations, and our flexibility of mind.

Thus our 'observation', or point of view, affects what we perceive as reality: in other words, we take part in creating our reality. It is very easy for people to limit themselves by only seeing what they choose to see. As William wrote after an experiment in transfiguration: 'It is all observation. There is no fixed reality.'

Other physical manifestations of energy were happening all the time. Often it seemed as if William, or the energy, was teasing us. Objects like spectacles, keys and pens frequently disappeared, reappearing later in another part of the room and sometimes not till the following week.

Quite early on we brought in a trumpet painted with a luminous band, an object traditionally used in seances. In March it not only began to roll around the table, but levitated and stayed in the air for about five minutes, then moved round the circle touching each member in turn. During the following weeks it floated, swung in time to the music on the cassette player, and one evening put on a whirling performance in the air, ending with a joint levitation with the table; we all broke into spontaneous applause!

On that occasion Brenda Marshall was present as a visitor. It was a particularly active evening; Brenda witnessed not only the jumping table and dancing trumpet but the materialisation of oil and the writing of numerous messages. One of these messages was: 'There is much PK [psychokinesis] which is misinterpreted as discarnate', confirming our belief that these phenomena were produced by mental energy rather than spirits. Brenda, normally rather reticent, declared herself very impressed.

Another evening all kinds of things were moved about including the trumpet, a handbell, the chairs, the cassette player and even myself. At the end of the session we were still sitting in darkness when a shuffle and a thump were heard. I had been moved, in my chair, three feet from the table. It was very odd; the switch was instantaneous and, although the thump seemed to indicate that I and my chair had been physically moved from one place to another, I had no sensation of my hands leaving the table or of any kind of motion.

From the early months our combined energies produced several apports, objects apparently brought magically from elsewhere. The first was in May, when some pot-pourri suddenly appeared on the writing pad. When Roger asked where it had come from William wrote: 'All reality is what you see. Where? is not a question. There is no where.'

We were often given flowers, most of which appeared instantaneously. Once they had arrived, they behaved like normal flowers, and we took them home and put them in vases. On 11 June we had another guest from the College staff. A bunch of sixteen cut pinks appeared for her, with a written message: 'Here is a present for Susan.' Overwhelmed and delighted, she asked where they had come from and was told: 'A present from the chaos which is condensed into an observation. The flowers are always here but now you can see them.' One evening we saw a single flower actually in the process of forming. By the light of the luminous tape around the trumpet Karen and I saw a kind of mist forming and slowly condensing. The trumpet then moved towards Trudy. We switched on the torch and saw that a single pink had materialised inside the trumpet's mouth.

The traditional spiritualist belief is that apports are transported to the seance by the spirit world from somewhere else, where they are already in existence. William's explanations were somewhat different. 'In what we are calling the state of probability of Infinite Mind, everything exists everywhere in some form. All we are doing is changing your perception. You don't have to move objects through time and space in order to apport them. You just adjust, if you like, the space and time of perception.'

We were learning about the importance of perception, and the need to go beyond 'rational' understandings. Because our rational minds can only associate motion with an object moving from one place to another, which is how the material universe works, it is natural to assume that when an object appears in a room it has travelled from elsewhere. In fact, there is a dimension in which the flowers exist in one particular place; but there is also a dimension of probability in which they are in a state of pure potential from which they could manifest anywhere. Since our minds can have access to more than one dimension, changing our observation between dimensions brings the flowers into the place where we observe them.

We also experimented with transfiguration, another phenomenon well known in spiritualism. Usually it consists of the medium's features and sometimes voice taking on those of a dead person, and some spiritualists regard it as important evidence for the survival of the personality. Our purpose, however, was to demonstrate how someone with a strong psychic energy can create recognisable faces through the power of thought.

We had some quite dramatic results. Whichever of us was being transfigured was observed by the rest of the group to undergo changes of features, often into an image chosen by someone else, on at least two occasions without announcing the choice aloud. The rest of the group were able to observe the subject's features transfiguring into the image chosen. These transfigurations included a Chinese 'guide', an American Indian 'guide', an old man, a young person, and even a hand which clearly had half a finger missing.

We were not bringing through a 'spirit personality', but simply changing our appearance. This was an objective physical perception: our faces did physically change, though our sense of ourselves did not, and the people being transfigured would feel a cobwebby sensation over their faces as their features altered.

We, of course, were choosing to create these thought-forms. But for people who are unaware of the underlying mechanisms such phenomena can be very disturbing, and have led to all kinds of beliefs in evil spirits, demonic possession and the like. During this time I saw a quite horrendous example of transfiguration unintentionally created by the victim as a result of religious conditioning.

I was called, via the college, to a house where poltergeist phenomena were taking place. They involved a young woman who had had a very strict Catholic upbringing, and had started when she agreed to sleep with her boyfriend. The first time they got into bed together all the covers were pulled off, the bed was tipped up, and the would-be lover fell out. When he got in again the whole bed shook and the bedclothes were again pulled off. In the end he ran off, totally terrified.

The phenomena carried on quite horrifically, with the furniture flying, rappings on the walls and bad smells, and the young woman assumed that the Devil had come to get her because of her wickedness. In fact she had a very powerful psychic energy, which had been triggered to produce poltergeist phenomena by her overwhelming sense of guilt.

Under circumstances like these I have to show that I

am not afraid – I have no need to be. As well as having a very powerful inner protection, I understand what I am dealing with. (However, should any of my readers encounter a poltergeist I do not recommend trying to deal with it as I do; poltergeists can be extremely scary.) After hearing the story, I did what I always do when faced with threatening energies. I said: 'All right, if there is anyone there and you've got any guts, show yourself!'

Instantly the young woman's face took on a devilish appearance. Her features transfigured into a typical representation of a demon, even down to the red eyes. The change was horrific.

I simply stood my ground, repeating, 'I am not afraid of you, I don't believe you are what you say you are. So just pack it in! You don't impress me.' Eventually the transfiguration subsided, and I was able to explain to the young woman what had happened. I advised her to have both healing and counselling to help overcome her guilt.

I am not saying that evil spirits don't exist; but although they may seem to have an objective, sometimes very powerful reality, they are simply the result of an interplay of perceptions. In fact, I do not believe there is any such thing as objective reality; rather, at some level of mind the human race has agreed to experience the same things within our physical universe, and within our accepted bounds of normality.

Thought-forms can stay around for centuries, becoming more and more powerful. Mind energy cannot be destroyed, but the thought-forms it creates can be altered. These demonic thought-forms, constructed by various belief systems over the centuries, can have an existence in another dimension, and fear and guilt can bring them into apparent reality in this one. They can, however, be changed into positive thought-forms or returned to pure energy. As was to become very clear through channelling, one purpose of the influx of Source Energy on this planet today is to help us release ourselves from the heavy burden of old, negative thought-forms, so that we are free to move on and evolve spiritually.

That year was very exciting for all of us. We were witnessing a range of phenomena rarely seen by any single group, and those whose background was in spiritualism were having to do some radical rethinking. For myself, I felt it very important to be bringing together a group which I knew was going to be vital for my future work. We were becoming very close, and we often met together socially as well as on our Monday evenings. This was another area of my life in which Chris was not involved. Although she had come to an early session as a visitor, it was simply not her kind of activity.

During that first year we saw many extraordinary things; as my Voice said at the time: 'Whatever you see may have an importance and often does, but you must add to it either the words or the energy of what it means to you. The phenomenon alone is not enough.'

We were, in fact, building up the group energy for the more important work of channelling the message from the Source, the message I had come to bring.

10

Channelling
from the
Source

Channelling is becoming an increasingly popular means of accessing higher wisdom and guidance. My Voice defines it as:

> a method of communication which enables the person doing the channelling – to a greater or lesser extent according to the medium's ability – to access information contained within wider intelligence. It is a link which at the moment is more readily accepted by the majority of people who will come to such mediums for the time being until they have the ability themselves to access the intelligence.

Nowadays when I channel for individuals I prefer to describe it as spiritual guidance, partly to distinguish myself from people who channel 'guides' who exist only within the Vortex. Even after I started channelling, my Voice continued for a long time to be nameless. (The name 'William' had been given to the group simply because our minds initially expected an individual personality.) This is important. People are accustomed to mediums channelling 'spirit guides' with Chinese or American Indian names (and often accents), whom they assume have lived with these identities on earth.

The words I channel are those of the Voice that has always spoken to me, which is in fact the Source. I am not channelling an individual but opening the doors to Source Energy, enabling it to speak. There are also other people with similar gifts to myself who are channelling the Source.

Listeners must use their discrimination and judge by the quality of the information they are given. The words channelled by mediums may come from the minds of people who have lived, but they may simply come from an aspect of the medium's own mind. And while many 'spirit guides' speak a lot of spiritual sense, there is always a danger of a personality cult growing up around a particular guide, which in the long run is limiting.

There is an anecdote circulating in the spiritualist world about a well-known medium who had channelled the same wise being for thirty years. While she was in trance, her guide was asked: 'Why is it always you who comes through?' The 'guide' replied, through the medium's mouth, 'Because my medium is too narrow-minded to take anybody else.'

The Energy that speaks through me and others like myself may be given names for convenience, but should not be confused with human personalities, groups of spirits or discarnate people, nor with most people's concept of God. When the Source expresses itself as 'we', as it often does, this is purely to indicate that it is not an individual speaking.

The Source has described itself as 'a singular point of infinity outside time and space': 'It is a timeless, universal perception, beyond all ideas of other spheres and levels, which has been translated in history, usually wrongly, as mythical lands. It goes beyond all ideas of other spheres and levels.' It is a state of consciousness where all probabilities exist and from which all mind originates. It is difficult for human beings to imagine this unlimited state because our entire experience is confined within our physical system, which itself is confined within a limited Vortex. I shall have more to say about the relationship between the Source and the Vortex in Chapter 12. For the moment, suffice it to repeat that the Source has its being outside the Vortex, and until it has evolved further the human mind will not be able to see beyond the Vortex.

William's written messages were of course a form of channelling, though slower and more laborious than the spoken word. They became more serious as they challenged members' conditioned beliefs on subjects like time, spirits, God and the future, and began to reveal the true purpose of the group: 'You are important in selecting the future from infinite probabilities. That is why the circle has been manifested.' We were told that at this crucial time in the evolution of humanity and the planet, it was the role of our group (among many others) to help people to see that the future is not fixed or predetermined. The future is always in a state of probability. By helping people to change their perception of reality, we could help to select the most creative potential future.

There had recently been an earthquake in Iran when we were told: 'When human beings have lost their sense of connection with the consciousness of the living earth this negative energy finds the weaknesses in the planet and it can erupt and break. There is much disruption and breakdown of structures near. The earth repays.

The Source is here to try and help this.' Many people are predicting nothing but catastrophes in the near future, and we had already been cautioned against making such predictions. Since thought is creative, predictions can be self-fulfilling, and as we approach the end of the century too many people are filling the minds of the public with portents of doom and gloom. As William explained: 'All energy has infinite probabilities. The selection of the correct ones is crucial. The creation of the universe is not one event. It is continuously happening in infinite ways.'

Predictions must not be confused with prophecy. Prophecy is an indication of how things might be, but is not an absolute forecast of what will happen. It offers us the opportunity of taking part in creating the future. If people put too much energy into believing a prediction, that belief may bring that prediction into reality. But as William told us, we have free choice.

There are infinite probabilities available. Free choice allows different futures to be selected. For every so-called event there are alternatives. One blink of an eye changes the universe.

It must be remembered that for the individual mind, the *observing* of an event *is* the event. The appearance of being a passive bystander watching things go past is only a model that is needed to make sense of experience. Each observation is a quantum package. The sensation of links between events is apparent because within the individual mind is an essence of Universal Mind which knows that all probable scenarios are contained at the point of singularity, where there is no separation between space and time.

The important thing for the growing mind is to

have its observation opened, to understand that reality is not a fixed state outside its observation but is part of their act of viewing it. The significance for an individual is to no longer feel that reality is a prison. This applies to any situation that must be faced. Pure acceptance of fate is to fix a point of observation and condense it into a solid mass.

I first channelled to the group in July 1990. I made no special preparation beforehand – you could say that my whole life had been the preparation. I had spent it listening to my Voice; now I was to share it with others.

That evening, everyone commented that the room was full of energy. Some people saw dim lights and flashes, the table moved without anyone touching it, and two of the group heard a kind of metallic whistling noise coming from the trumpet. After some communications from William I sat down in an armchair to go into a trance.

As I consciously linked my mind with the Source there was a great surge of energy and the trumpet flew from the floor into the air, falling back to the floor on the other side of the table. The next moment, it seemed, I opened my eyes and was told that I had been speaking for about half an hour. I had been totally in trance and heard nothing of what I said, though I had a sense of the content. Of course I listened to the tape afterwards.

When I began channelling I always went into a trance state. From one point of view this has a psychological advantage, in that when I am in trance my hearers seem to listen more attentively and quietly; however, now that channelling has become very much part of my working life I no longer need to go into trance. When I speak to small groups, I just close my eyes and become the Source instantly.

That first evening's message began with an answer to a question from Roger on the nature of the group:

> This group was chosen to come together a long time before many of us even knew each other. There are members who are very specifically from the Source, and some who will not be directly aligned to it, but will be part of its work here. This is not a two-tier or any kind of system which means that one is less than the other. It is a coming together of levels necessary to bring into a society that is desperately in need an energy which has been missing for some time.
>
> Those who are aligned directly to the circle have had implanted into them at some crisis in their life an energy of the Source. It has been put in when they have been most able to accept it. Each of those here who are aligned have had to have a crisis in which that energy was implanted.

One of the signs of Source Energy is that it has the ability to change matter, and to materialise energy into matter. There was at least one evening when everyone in the group found perfumed oil materialising in their hands. Everyone felt quite awed, and the shared experience brought us all closer together. It was very exciting for everyone to be given not only a sign of the Source, and its empowerment of the group, but to know that the work really was unfolding, that we were truly working together in a common cause.

In June, Karen had found oil spontaneously materialising in her hands at home, and William explained to us that it was because her Source Energy had a particularly close resonance with my own, enabling her to have similar experiences to myself, and that 'in your terms you have shared many incarnations'. Now the channelling confirmed that her energy was very similar to mine. The following week a quartz crystal cluster was apported for her, with the message: 'This is your link with another dimension.'

The channelling made it very clear, however, that having Source Energy did not make anyone superior or elite. Hierarchies and elites are human concepts, irrelevant in universal terms, and everyone was necessary to the group, like the pieces of a jigsaw. This was stressed more than once.

> Humans are obsessed with hierarchies. Hierarchy belongs only in your minds which need to order things. Being good at something does not make you a better person.

> Elitism is purely a human concept because human beings find it so hard to accept that some can have more than others without being superior. And it is a fact, some have something which is special, others do not. They are not superior by that – nor even better people. There is nothing wrong with ability. It is only when it becomes a method to encourage dislike and jealousy that it becomes a concept which is misunderstood. If you have a talent, if you have an ability, you should say that you have it and be proud and not hide it because others think you are an elite. That is their reality and their problem, not yours.

The role of everyone in our group was to unlock and open the eyes of those who were ready to discover that there is no reality other than that which we create, and to find their own power within them. It was to communicate and to change the reality of those who would listen to our message, and to open the minds of more and more people to the probability of a future in which humanity will evolve dramatically. There are many groups now working together to help the progress of this evolution. Some I know of personally, but I am aware that they exist all over the planet, some operating very quietly, some with a more public profile.

You are one of a whole series of groups working on this level – although you may not see all the results of your work. The results are to do with those who are willing to open their minds to see that they are taking part in the future, and can be more responsible for its creation.

One or two members will be standing up to be counted. One or two members will pay the cost of that because of the criticisms that will be thrown at them. The others are there to support and know that the truth is being given.

But you are not apprentice messiahs, you are not going to preach to the world and be sacrificed for the sins of others. It is a question of creating an energy which people can tap into if they wish, and which will become part of the evolutionary process. There are elements of each individual's brain which are collective, which is why so many people *en masse* see the same reality.

Some here know the probable futures that could happen. All that needs to be done is to avoid some of them. It mustn't be thought of as full of gloom, because none of this energy can be destroyed. There is already an infiltration beginning to happen, as more and more of this energy is making more and more so-called individuals begin to see that they do not have to accept that they are separate, or that they are absolutely unable to change their future.

We were being told that there is a definite opportunity for harmony here, a vibrant living force which can really bring about change for the good.

At this stage the work of the group had already altered the thinking and the work of some of its members. Trudy, for instance, was beginning to change the way she practised her mediumship. Roger had withdrawn completely from traditional mediumship in order to encompass his new perceptions, and was putting forward Source ideas in his psychic development classes. In my healing and in leading workshops and demonstrations of my work, I was also of course teaching Source ideas, trying to show a wider public that no one has to be limited by their beliefs.

One of the public demonstrations I carried out with the help of the College was to use mental energy to affect the electromagnetic energy of a cassette tape. I did this by *thinking* the words of a Dylan Thomas poem on to a sealed cassette tape. The experiment was carried out with care; three unopened cassettes were placed in the College safe, and a member of the staff designated which tape I was to use. Each evening at home, for about a week, I projected the thought of the poem to the tape, which was still in the safe.

On the night of the demonstration, a representative of the College took all three tapes to Friends' House, the Quaker central offices and meeting house in the Euston Road. The one on to which I had projected the poem was opened and played. There was a lot of static on it, but the audience could hear every word of the poem, enunci-ated very clearly in a slightly impersonal voice.

Tony Scofield was present at that demonstration; while not doubting my own integrity, he comments that a scientist could think up ways in which this could be fiddled by someone very determined. It would have to be a very elaborate fiddle. For Tony, although such feats are impressive, the repetitive work we did in the lab, under strictly controlled conditions, was far more convincing from the purely scientific point of view.

Trudy, however, was also there that evening to give clairvoyance, and she recognised just how powerful this demonstration was. The week before, she had seen me manifest vibhouti at Stevenage spiritualist church (there was another rush from the congregation to gather it up.) But the tape experiment struck her as even more remarkable. She told me later that, although the audience might not have realised just what they were witnessing, it was the most extraordinary thing she had seen me do.

I did not channel again until the autumn, but then began many evenings of channelling. Every member of the group channelled at least once, sometimes with a little difficulty at first as they learned to put aside their rational minds. We tape-recorded and transcribed all these sessions. With Brenda Marshall's encouragement I also began channelling similar information to small public groups at the College.

Some of this information related to the concept of God, making it even more clear that God is not to be confused with the Source, that the gods created by various reli-gions are in fact thought-forms existing entirely within the Vortex.

God, like all concepts, is dependent on your observation. There is no fixed god because all is evolving. At the point of singularity [i.e. the Source] all is one and infinite. . . . There is no fixed deity. . . . You all see God every day. There is no God when you do not see.

Man is God with loss of memory and is always frustrated because he knows there is more. He becomes angry and hurts. When man is God again the pain will pass.

God is merely your observation of a reality which you do not understand and cannot be put into logic and words. It is a method of trying to personify the energy and consciousness of your observable universe, which is a natural and innate quality of the matter which forms it. This is why it is possible to say there is no God and yet have an intelligence which is universal. For those who observe a God in the universe, God exists, but it becomes at the same time a closed universe with that God in it.

God guides those who need God to guide them: they are guiding themselves because the universe and the individuals are one. When there is an expansion which goes beyond the need to make a form of God, then mind will have escaped the prison of reality and move on.

[Escaping the prison of reality] is part of the quest now going on in which you as well as others are involved. It is the beginning of the new evolution of consciousness . . . learning how to continually work at removing all barriers and removing all structures until they begin to break down.

Another subject which was illuminated through channelling was death.

There is no death, only a ceasing of observing. Personality is energy and is not destructible. However the next life is not a place but an observance.

[After death], people are where they think they are. There is no other truth. Wherever they think they are in their time, that is where they are until they learn that they can go beyond the structure they have created. There is no spirit world. There is only that which their thoughts create.

We also received information on the nature of spiritual development, which may help to explain why, when we made our message public, it was not altogether well received:

The job of expanding minds is hard and you will despair at times. If one moves on, the universe is enhanced. Those who listen will expand. You can only speak. You cannot hear for them.

Teaching development is no longer to do with the individual's growth but is tapping the necessary changes that have happened to what we may refer to as the planetary soul.

Try to conceive an idea of the whole planet as an organism which has a spirit. The planetary spirit has evolved very markedly. It has changed the energies and will reflect in the physical manifestations on the planet.

The object of the teaching must be to encourage every single member never to close or confine their reality, their observation or consciousness, but be prepared to stretch it further and further. That every time they find that they have individualised it, or have formed a concept or an idea, to use it, then to dissipate it and find what is behind it.

The beginning of channelling marked a shift towards the profounder spiritual purpose of our work. Putting into words the meaning of Source Energy and its presence here brought it into greater reality, allowing the knowledge to enter the minds of the group. Since humanity and this planet are about to undergo enormous changes, it is necessary for more and more people to understand the nature of this Energy, which should not be seen as occult or mystic but as real and powerful and spiritual and usable, and a necessary part of our evolution.

11

Conflict and Change

The year 1990 was a very eventful one. I not only grew in understanding and abilities, but what could be called a spiritual awakening was accompanied by some deep soul-searching and a major emotional upheaval. Spiritual development unfortunately doesn't consist of simply floating through life sweetly unfolding and spreading love and light. It is more like a birth process which demands going through realistic, tough emotional contractions to bring the new being into reality. During this year I was having to acknowledge my own role as a representative of Source Energy, and the transition was not always easy.

Now that the transitional phase is complete I accept it; I don't feel arrogant at talking about my gifts. Arrogance is of course objectionable, but I think a lot of people could benefit from acknowledging their gifts without feeling they have to play them down. There is nothing wrong with honest self-evaluation. Society, particularly British society, still affected by centuries of guilt-laden religion, has conditioned us to feel more comfortable saying we are miserable, worthless sinners than acknowledging what we really are. That's a load of nonsense. Miserable we might be on occasion, but worthless sinners we are not.

However, in the autumn of 1990 I was still adjusting to my role. Once I started channelling, it was as if the Energy that had always sat within me was telling me, 'We are not separate, we are becoming each other.' My whole structure and outlook were going through a complete revolution, and this inevitably had repercussions on my private life.

There is a general expectation in the public's mind that people like myself should be both perfect and above earthly troubles. Neither is true. Being within a human experience has been my choice, and learning to deal with human emotions and fallibility has been a necessary part of that choice, since I am here to communicate with human beings. But this has meant that the road towards declaring what I am, despite my inner sense of certainty, has not been an easy one – for me, or for those close to me. I am not like some celibate priest advising people on their marriages. I am not removed from the experiences and difficulties and conflicts that other people have. I have had to go through them before I could shed them.

Now I was beginning to realise that the role I had undertaken was going to be very demanding, and would place me in a position of responsibility. My sense of purpose began to over-ride all other considerations, including Chris's needs. Our relationship was still in many ways extraordinary, but it seemed to me that what we each wanted as individuals could never balance.

Part of the conflict arose because Chris had no way of understanding what was going on within me. It was hard to explain to her, and I don't think I tried very hard. The very powerful inner experience of Source Energy was something she could not share. It was as if the energy within me wouldn't let go. Sometimes I would even say to it, 'Go away and leave me alone – I want to be happy with Chris. We've got a good relationship and I don't want to throw it away.' At times I felt torn to pieces and deeply depressed.

Chris was very long-suffering; when she complained, it was in the kindest way. She would say, 'I understand about the work, but you must make time for *you*.' I am sure she was right, but we had different priorities. At one point I said quite openly to her, 'Of course you're important, but the only thing in my life that's really important is my work.' I convinced myself that my single-mindedness was totally justified.

So while beautiful things were happening in my work, my relationship with Chris was finally ending. For several months I suffered psychological and emotional turmoil. I felt very isolated and Chris found it hard to communicate with me. I realised that I was spending less and less time with her, and I knew that was hard for her. Yet I couldn't, or wouldn't, change my behaviour. After all the support she had given me she must have felt very rejected.

The conflict grew worse when I started asking myself what I really wanted and how I really felt: did I still love Chris, and what does love mean anyway? It was all very complicated, and very painful for both of us.

My relationship with Chris was like meeting someone in the middle of a maze, without knowing where I was. The feelings I had for her were more powerful than any I had experienced before. With her I had been able to express insecurities and doubts that I had been harbouring for years, but also a love I could pour out without restraint. The journey from the centre of the maze was coloured by powerful, often conflicting feelings – elation, an exchange of minds, blind alleys, anger and frustration. This shared journey, which at one time I thought would never have to end, culminated in two different exits – one for each of us.

I finally came to the conclusion that I really ought to get away. A friend found me somewhere to stay, and I moved out. But that solved nothing, and after a few days I went back, in a state of unhappy confusion. At one point I wondered, 'Do I have to be alone to do this work? Maybe I can't have relationships.' For a short time I decided that was probably the answer. As it turned out, I was wrong.

I knew I must talk to someone. I had a good friend in the group, Karen, who shared my knowledge of Source Energy and had a similar outlook on life. And we had of course been told through channelling that we had shared Source Energy in the past. Karen, I thought, might be able to help me to clarify my confusion. I asked her to meet me and we went for a meal at a local pub.

I was never a heavy drinker, and a couple of glasses of wine had the effect of taking the lid off my feelings. My attention had originally been drawn to Karen because of her energy, and its resonance with mine. Now we both realised that, although we had hardly ever been alone together, a human attraction and attachment had been building up between us, unrecognised and unspoken until now. Once we acknowledged our feelings, it was like opening up a sealed box. One moment we were good friends who shared a major interest; the next we were lovers.

I had left Chris with the intention of sorting things out: I never returned. For myself, moving in with Karen, which I speedily did, was absolutely right; we harmonised so well on all levels that I was no longer torn in half. From Chris's point of view, the suddenness of what can only have felt like a betrayal must have been a shock, and I suspect that some of the friends we shared in those days still blame me.

At the time I just walked away, leaving the 'goodbyes' in the air, which I regret very much. Since then, I have learnt that when a relationship ends goodbyes are necessary. Despite my happiness with Karen, it was a long time before I resolved my feelings of regret about Chris; writing about her (with her permission) has made me look again at what happened, and to say the goodbye I did not say at the time.

This major move, in December 1990, was followed in January by a further upheaval when the Monday night circle ran into trouble with the College authorities.

The psychic world is unfortunately rife with competitiveness, particularly within large organisations. Their very structure creates a setting in which, rather than rejoicing in their shared gifts, mediums, psychics and healers feel threatened by any colleague who appears more talented, successful or glamorous than themselves, or who promulgates new ideas. And when people feel threatened, they attack.

In my own case I was doing things that others couldn't, things in the realms of the miraculous. I could materialise oils, aromatic ash and objects, and also dematerialise them. (At one public lecture at the College I placed some cress seeds in a woman's hand and closed her fingers into a fist. All the seeds disappeared.) In addition I was still the only healer in the College with my own room, I was in demand by patients, I had been reported in the newspapers. I was running a group with special privileges and a closed membership.

Although Brenda Marshall had given us every support, there were undercurrents in the College that were less than supportive. So far they had amounted to no more than a few grumbles about our special treatment. One of the younger psychics, an excellent channel, had complained that I was allocated more than my fair share of workshops. We had also had one complaint from a medium, working late in the room beneath ours, about the noise of the table jumping about; after that we started later in the evening, to be sure we would disturb no one. Otherwise I ignored any rumours, since no one confronted me directly.

Then, on 14 January 1991, when we had been meeting for just over a year, Brenda Marshall invited us to give a lecture about our work at the College. It was exciting; even though some of the phenomena had been produced a hundred years before, I knew that what we had to say about them would create quite a stir – just how much, I did not foresee. The College's publicity for our talk, entitled 'New Forms of Physical Phenomena', announced that the results of our circle at the CPS 'have surpassed all expectations and communications have been received which open new dimensions'.

We presented the lecture as a group. Roger described the logistics of our meetings, while Karen talked about our experiments and their implications for our understanding of time, space and reality. Trudy spoke about the group's effect on her approach to mediumship, and I talked about the channelled philosophy, including the imminent breakdown of structures, and how our new understanding of the nature of reality affected our views on concepts such as guides, God and the spirit world.

Our immediate reception was very positive. The hall was filled to overflowing and we left to rapturous applause. Brenda Marshall expressed great enthusiasm and told us that the talk would be published in the next issue of the College journal, *Light*.

At our next meeting, the following Monday, we were told: 'Another strand of the group's work has already commenced, and that is by virtue of presenting to many more minds the concepts that are written about. This represents only one avenue. There is coming near a new reality. Do not feel because you are small in number that you are small in effect. This energy is infinite. You are infinite.'

Within a week we were told that the group was no longer welcome at the College. Immediately after the lecture, one or two of the staff had begun making their discontent known. Some people had worked at the College for years without spring-cleaning their ideas, and our approach caused them great discomfort – an attitude I found surprising within an organisation which I had understood to offer an open forum for discussion and exploration.

One of our more contentious views concerned creative reality. I am certainly not the only contemporary speaker in this field to suggest that thought is creative, but I go perhaps further than some. I know for myself that everything exists in a state of probability; the reality that we observe at any one time is only a portion of the whole.

Some people misinterpreted this view as 'nothing exists', and one medium accused me of nihilism. Far from being nihilistic, I was actually saying that *everything* exists in a state of potential, and can be brought into being by our perception. This means that the spirit world is just one of many potential states within the Vortex. We should not assume, because somebody comes through after death with a description of 'the other side', that that is how the afterlife is for everyone, and for ever. Their perception is real and valid, but it may be just a part of the potential, not the only possibility.

Perhaps not surprisingly, some of our information

about the nature of guides and spirit communications caused some discomfort to an audience full of mediums. This particularly applied to my belief that some mediums become so secure in their relationship with a particular guide – who may be no more than the wishful creation of their own higher minds – that they lack the courage to let go of it and move on. As William had told us, reverence for one's guide can be a prison.

Sticking to the known is safe; however, it may mean that some mediums are transmitting no more than thought-forms which they have helped to create, rather than producing new, expanding, evolving information. We were not suggesting that our audience was wrong, but rather that they should take a new look at their beliefs, and that there could be a different view of reality.

The backlash came swiftly. Within a few days I had a meeting with Brenda Marshall who told me reluctantly that there were some problems; a number of people, including some members of the College Council, were not happy about some of the things I had said. One medium had even stated that he could see 'dark energy' around me, 'misleading people'. Without further discussion, she told me that the Council had decided the group must leave, and I must henceforth restrict my activities in the College to healing. This struck me as totally illogical; if I was really influenced by 'dark forces' I should surely not be healing the sick!

The group moved out immediately. For a time I continued giving healing at the College, but I felt it was important to address some of the comments that had been made. Eventually, after several meetings, the Council wrote to me admitting that the fact that a clairvoyant saw something was not absolute proof of its existence.

By now, however, I had had enough; I had no wish to go on working in a place where my activities could be censored. And I was shocked that the encouragement we had received could be turned upside down overnight. Now I cut all my ties with the College, as did Roger, who was unwilling to compromise.

I know that some of the information given by the Source is bound to produce the kind of reaction we had experienced. Much of my work is about the breakdown of structures, and we had been speaking to a very structured organisation. Later that year William wrote succinctly: 'Every structure is either a rung on a ladder or a room without a door – choice.... Structure is a tool, not an edifice.' This was exactly how the College appeared to me: like a closed room. At that time, no one there seemed to be building ladders. Mental structures and doctrines are thought-forms which become reality to those who uphold them. Blindly following dogmatic belief systems, particularly those that promise some kind of salvation to those who obey their rules, totally undermines the self-empowerment of the believers. These systems become mental and emotional prisons which ultimately create conflict. For the human race to evolve, these structures will have to break down: in fact this process has started. We are already seeing it happening in our political and economic systems, and within various Churches and religions.

Getting out of the College proved to be one of the best things I ever did. It gave me the space to work as I needed to, free of structures imposed by others. The College has been through its own changes since then, among them the appointment of a new President.

While the move freed the group from restraints and censorship, it also sowed the seeds of further change:

looking back, the break with the College heralded the end of this particular group. Eventually Roger, Rosemary and Trudy were to withdraw to follow their individual paths. But, with occasional guests, we continued to meet for over a year at Roger and Rosemary's flat, where some even more powerful phenomena and channelling took place.

At the time, although Karen and I were quite happy about the move, the others were somewhat shaken. As William wrote that summer: 'We can assure you that all change causes resistance. Big change – big resistance.' It was no small thing for Roger and Rosemary to leave the College where they had worked for many years, and it seemed very unfair after all the praise they had received. Trudy made staunch efforts to convey our philosophy to other spiritualist groups, and met with some criticism for her pains. She was still working at the College as a medium, but with the expanded knowledge she had gained in the group. William had always encouraged her to continue giving sittings because of their value to the sitters, and she passed her interpretations of the teachings to those who were receptive to them. William advised her: 'As long as you are aware of sources of information, you can be clairvoyant. Clairvoyance is only looking at all probabilities and trying to present clearly that which gives a choice to the sitter. Grandmothers exist when you observe, use them.'

On our first evening at the Stones' flat, Roger told William he was glad he had made the transition. William replied: 'Welcome. We are pleased to be here or there!' We had been discussing the possibility of writing the history of the group, and the pen now wrote: 'No constraints on work. You can publish it. Have no fear. If time existed, this would be a new era.'

At the next meeting we were told that, since truth is relative, our philosophy must not be preached as a doctrine but put forward as ideas to be explored. As William once wrote: 'I do not teach, I only open doors.' The messages from the Source are not to be understood as yet another dogma in which people must believe in order to be saved.

> This is not about absolute truths, it is about the importance of perspective and observing. It is too easy – and this has been done throughout history with religious writings – to extract and take small parts of anything that is said and use it in argument to try and put up a barrier and/or a doctrine.
> We warned you that all this work would become controversial and would alarm and upset some people. People merely take that which they choose to take in order to defend those truths that they have made absolute, instead of relative.

In May we received some important teachings which were triggered when Karen asked for some practical details about the new evolutionary consciousness. With beautiful simplicity, the pen wrote:

> Awareness of inter-dimension.
> Care about nature.
> Energy manipulation for good intent.
> Creating a good god who will end the churches, cast down the stones and demolish the pious.

Karen asked whether we could find any way of communicating this philosophy to others without causing gross offence?

'No,' wrote William.

'Are you suggesting we "publish and be damned"?'
'Yes.'
'When?'
'You decide. You have the power.'

At the end of May William returned to the subject of publishing our work, and we began discussing the format of a possible book. 'Do not analyse yet, we have more to give. Just start getting it together,' we were instructed. In fact, there was so much more to give that, although we continued to keep our records, I did not start work on this book until 1992.

In May and June more information was channelled to us about the evolution of consciousness:

There is a conscious evolution in your terms of time moving the whole of the planet forward. It is not in fact new because it is already with you. In your so-called past many have glimpsed it, and have been called prophets. But they have interpreted it in such a way that it has been misunderstood. The essence of prophets and prophecy is not foretelling. Their interpretation may be wrong in the sense of being a series of events which will come true, but the glimpse of knowledge is not. They are seeing potentials, which they understand can be brought into existence. Therefore the prophecies of many religions speak of new millennia, of God coming and changing the earth and of stars falling from the sky.

All these are merely symbols of a misunderstood dimension. The new millennium simply means that the human consciousness will know that it is God already, that humans do not need to create a being to do it for them. That realisation will be part of the new consciousness and that will be the new growth. Much of this spiritual understanding has been entrapped in narrow doctrines, and it is time for it to be released.

When, again in time order and in your terms, the day arrives that the evolution of consciousness takes place, all the concepts of pain and suffering and emotions of all kinds will no longer have the same meaning and significance as they do now.

The work of the Source is to be apparent so that for those with consciousness in the individual form, again in time terms, the evolutionary pathway to achieve this will be awakened and the evolutionary change will take place. This cannot be expected to happen in the span of one lifetime; it will take generations to complete.

Human beings, we were told, potentially have an awareness of the entire energy of the universe. The fact that most people only experience individual awareness creates an inner conflict; they feel incomplete, knowing somehow that there is more but finding it hard to connect with that potential. The resultant sense of separation has given rise to the myths about fallen angels and the division into heaven and hell.

This perception is now changing. This is why institutions built upon these concepts will crumble. This is why the Churches, with their doctrinised structure... which has built that perception into a complete theology, will disappear forever. They will fall, make no mistake. That future is now selected. They have sown the seeds of their own destruction. This must be seen not as a step backwards, but as a positive step into the light that is within.

During that summer we resumed an earlier, uncompleted experiment of actually bringing the Source Energy into the room as a tangible force, so that the whole group could experience it. My role was to be the focus of all those present, so that my Source Energy could be made external while my physical body was sustained by the energy of the group. At the start, as I went into trance, the room seemed extraordinarily dark. In this utter, infinite blackness Trudy, Karen and I saw stars and patterns of light all around us; Trudy felt as if she was out in space.

After preparation and meditation, the Source Energy was released and we could all hear, from different parts of the room, a sound like the ticking of a clock, which appeared to slow down. (It was explained afterwards through channelling that this was a symbol of the group being enclosed in a time capsule, in which the time we were experiencing was slowed down relative to the time outside it.) Then, although the air around us remained quite still, the room was filled with the sound of a rushing wind, symbolising the Source Energy.

This was one of the most powerful experiences the group had shared. It was followed by a long, long silence. It was the kind of happening beyond human emotion to which it was impossible to put words. It gave us all the profound feeling of being part of something both wonderful and immense. Karen commented afterwards that, although it was extraordinary, it was a confirmation of what she had already known within her.

At the next two sessions we were given information about our roles, including advice to move forward, to be self-reliant, and not to fear change. I was told that the time to stand up again and be counted was coming.

I explained to the group that I had always been aware of my 'mission' ever since the Source Energy had been implanted in me, though not all the information was revealed at once. Now I understood that it had been necessary for me to search for the probabilities. Although I had been given work to do, mainly during the past three years, there was more to come. In a recent moment of joining with the Source I knew that the time had arrived: that the most important part of my life was to begin. I knew I could count on the support of Source groups and people, especially Karen. I knew that my mission had a limited timespan, and there would come a time when the Source would continue through others the work that I had begun.

I was now quite clear about the nature of my mission. It is to create Centres of Light where the message, the energy and the healing power of the Source can be offered to all those who wish to receive it. It is to give people the opportunity of changing their perception and liberating themselves from internal prisons to release their full potential. It is to open up new energies, so that those who are receptive to them can understand that there is a major evolutionary change available for good, and for harmony, and that they can take part in bringing it into being.

12

The Vortex

I was still going through personal changes and adjustments, and I was fortunate to be with Karen. She was going through changes of her own, and understood their implications both on a personal level and in our work. By the autumn our relationship was well established. We had settled down together in Ealing in West London, where I spent my days giving healing and channelling from home. Karen continued with her job; her psychic gifts have not followed the same path as mine, since she channels and teaches spiritual development rather than doing public or healing work. She also supports me in my public excursions into workshops and channelling to groups.

Karen was not only a great support – she turned out to be the only woman I had ever met whom I could not beat in an argument. This came as quite a blow; the first time it happened I was devastated. It took me some time, but I have eventually learnt to accept it. Of course, when I am in my Source Energy winning or losing is not an issue; I am now beginning to learn to apply to everyday life what I would naturally apply to the rest of my work.

Something else that is new in our relationship is that, although human emotions can be so all-consuming, I have always been aware that in physical terms they are transient. With Karen that no longer feels true, since I know that we both come from and will return to the same Source.

We married in September 1991 and spent our honeymoon in Turkey. William apported some freesias for us, with the written message: 'It's not a bouquet but best wishes.' The Monday before our wedding, he told us: 'The jigsaw is complete. The picture is of eternal and dimensional happiness. . . . If we may be old hat, many blessings.'

That autumn the group held one or two small workshops, demonstrating energy phenomena like table-moving and germinating cress seeds. One of my aims was to get over people's fears that such activities are somehow spiritualistic, to make it clear that they have very little to do with spirits and very much to do with the power of the mind.

We also put on a large workshop in London at Friends' House in Euston Road. I wanted to see whether we could produce similar results with the general public and whether this was an appropriate way to get people to attune to energy. As a demonstration of psychokinetic energy it was very successful. Tables were levitating and shooting round the room, and people were rendered nearly weightless so that they could be lifted with virtually no effort. I also accelerated the growth of cress seeds and showed how I could move a pendulum sealed in a jar without touching it. Most of the group came and there was an enormous amount of positive energy in the room.

Although it was very successful, as well as enjoyable in itself, I did not repeat it. Energised tables surprise people, but they do not lift them into a higher dimension or open their minds to the realms of deeper meaning that can be brought about by the manifestation of oil or crystals.

Throughout 1991 the content of the Monday night groups had become more concerned with serious information and less with phenomena. In August, Karen was channelling when the subject of the proposed book came up again. We were told:

> We are anxious it should be published in the near future.... There will be an emphasis on channelling to complete the information you already have.... In the first instance there will be a single publication. It would be of great benefit if additional material could be published subsequently. It will not be possible to release all the information which is to be communicated all at a single time in a single publication.

During that evening's channelling we were given the most important information we had so far received. It was the group's introduction to the concept of the Vortex, and why our message is so necessary at this time. The reason we are in a state of planetary and spiritual crisis is that the system we live within has become cut off from Infinite Mind, of which it is a part. It is like a Vortex, a whirlpool, which has become so deep that instead of flowing back into the stream from which it originated it has become trapped within itself.

All this is of course an analogy; this is the only way in which this information can be conveyed, since we do not have the words or the mental concepts to encompass the actuality. But it is not difficult to envisage Infinite Mind as a stream which originated from the Source, and is only infinite when viewed from within the Vortex. But it is like a timeless river constantly flowing with no beginning and no end, giving rise to eddies and whirlpools of consciousness, which then return back to the flow of the stream.

The Vortex we are in is like one of these many whirlpools. It is a creative force, since it originates in Infinite Mind, and it has created everything within itself, without requiring a God or divine plan. From our own, relative point of view it contains infinite potential, and one of the potentials it has realised is our universe, including the planet on which we live and all its life-forms, as well as all the other dimensions we can contact.

However, instead of returning to the stream, as it needs to do, the Vortex has become a self-observing, closed system. Conscious only of itself, it has lost its connection with its origins. The planet, the universe, all the thought-forms within our dimension and unseen dimensions, including concepts such as the spirit world and reincarnation, are the necessary creations of a consciousness enclosed within itself. To human minds, these creations may seem infinite; they appear as levels and planes and hierarchies of existence, but they are all inside the confines of the Vortex. And so long as they are trapped inside it, their evolution is limited. They are isolated from the stream to which they truly belong.

Now the problem becomes very difficult if the consciousness within one Vortex has become self-observing to the point where it has become dislocated from the stream. It can then only perceive within the Vortex. This has two major effects. The first is a belief that all the perceptions of the material universe and other dimensions within the Vortex are all that exists.

The Vortex has become a fragment broken off from the stream of consciousness. Fragmentation then becomes the norm for that conscious observance and it begins to see everything in fragments or compartments. Consciousness within the Vortex divides up not only the whole universe but the whole of its mental processes into separate units which seem to have no connection.

It is as if people are seeing a separateness in everything, which is not actually real. When this perception becomes a fixed, solid pattern, it appears that the material of the universe is separate from human consciousness, when in fact it is a part of it.

Therefore, for example, the planet upon which the human minds live is seen as a fragment of rock which has upon it separate natural processes which evolve from one another but which do not exist in one stream: and the importance of one to the other becomes lost.

There is here almost a paradox, in that the members of a single species, originating from one stream of conscious energy, behave as if they are a series of separate entities and enter into conflict with each other. The species is in fact in conflict with itself.

All this has become more and more isolated until co-existence within the Vortex has become almost impossible. Social, political or any of the other human methods of realignment cannot alone supply the answer unless they also address the need for every individual to evolve back into Infinite Mind. True spiritual self-empowerment is the key.

The second point is that when a Vortex becomes fixed, as well as the effects within it, there is also an effect on the flow of Infinite Mind itself, just as a whirlpool alters the whole flow of the stream around it.

This means that all the dimensions contained within that stream can no longer flow in what you would call infinite probability but must always encounter the Vortex and adjust accordingly. The fixed Vortex is affecting the stream, which is consciousness as a whole. This is why it is so important that change must occur, so that evolution will go on and not be interfered with.

Many will ask 'Why has this happened?', implying that there is some kind of omnipotent power ensuring that nothing ever goes wrong. In reality there is no omnipotent force overlooking all events. Consciousness has infinite probability and therefore great promise, but it is not totally regulated so that everything becomes perfect. It is a spontaneous creative force, and the true power lies within every individual. You do not have to look for 'why?' when there are infinite ways to evolve and learn.

The idea that there is no omnipotent power all set to save us at the last minute comes as a shock to some people – even to those who no longer believe in conventional religion. When I am channelling to new listeners, many of them jump to the conclusion that the Source is synonymous with an all-powerful God, who will rescue the 'saved' from destruction. The Source is a point of infinite being, a state of infinite potential from which everything possible arises. But while it is beyond human imagining, it is not omnipotent in the sense of being able to direct human events.

I am often asked about the relationship of the Source to Infinite Mind. The two are not identical. Once again, I can only use analogies. But we can envisage the Source as the parent of the stream of Infinite Mind. As in human terms, a child does not remain an extension of the parent, but has a life of its own. The Source exists outside the stream, aware of and concerned for it. But the nearest it can come to intervention is to enter the Vortex by implanting its energy into human beings like myself, in order to show people the way to free themselves. Our future depends not on any God, nor on the Source alone, but on our own co-operation with the Source.

The Vortex has become fixed and has stayed fixed. This has set up a pattern which has become so enmeshed that it now needs a change of conscious awareness to move it. The energy is being put in to try and adjust that observance so that it moves on back into its infinite probability, where it truly belongs. This is not like a hand coming in and totally taking over. It is, if you like, a gentle method of allowing the structures within the Vortex to become less rigid so that it will return to the stream, and all consciousness can then readjust.

People are going to find it hard to let go of their images of an all powerful God or purposeful creator who makes sure things happen. Yet they are faced with a paradox: they see a world fragmented, destroying itself, murdering itself, but they cling to an idea of a God who is looking after them, even when the events in front of their eyes must indicate that no such power exists. This is taking away the responsibility of the self-observing mind to go forward and become the God it already is.

God is not outside waiting to put things right. Every conscious awareness is God already, if you have to use that expression, and when it realises that and moves on, then consciousness will expand once more. This includes the gods of science, politics and all the other systems which currently separate consciousness.

[We must] realise that the work being carried on here, and in all the energy centres where this is being attempted, is not a work of saving the universe. If the plan (for want of a better word, because a plan implies an order) is to succeed, it is the energy being put into it which will ultimately bring it about. Not in a thunderous moment, not in a revelation from the sky when something will return to save the world, but, in your terms, a time period when the patterns set up for trying to change the energy, including a drastic realignment of the population of this planet as you observe it, will take place.

There is to be no judgment from the skies. No God will come down and judge the wicked or the good and cast people into a pit. All these ideas are self-observing limitations. The future is a good one if the potential is chosen, and the potential is being worked on now. There is hope and purpose in your terms, because purpose is part of your conscious energy. It is already ingrained within it, and the joy of spreading your minds and all minds across infinite probability, and discovering the wonder of creative reality in its true sense, will be a revelation which will need no God from the skies to give.

Here is a clear message that we can free ourselves, but it is up to everyone to participate in their own liberation. I as a Source representative cannot let you out, but I can help you to find your own way out. A major step towards human freedom is for us to release ourselves from the mental and social structures we ourselves have built, which imprison our spiritual nature. In many people this thought creates resistance, not to say fear, which is reflected in the current swing towards fundamentalism, racism, nationalism and other extremes.

These structures not only create a false security; they are also responsible for much human suffering. Suffering is not inflicted on us from outside; it is not a punishment from on high. It is the result of being trapped in an energy that we have failed to move out of. Once we travel through our fear and resistance, we will be able to sense the true freedom which is our spiritual birthright.

All this channelled information was already part of my own awareness and came as no surprise to me, but some of the group took a while to come to terms with its implications. Many people receive these ideas somewhat fearfully at first, but once they have absorbed them they find a great sense of liberation. Roger, for instance, was ultimately helped to release himself from a great deal of his past structured conditioning and to recognise the validity of his own perception. Trudy, part of whom was very comfortable with the secure spirit world, began to see the value of accepting what is really happening and what we can do about it. For Karen, it put into context ideas and concepts that she had had since childhood; she found it very exciting to have confirmation of ideas that she had glimpsed before without fully understanding them.

The week after receiving this channelling we began the session by discussing among ourselves the breakdown of structures that is needed for our evolution. The pen wrote its own comment: 'We have to accept that history has built many walls. Each stone has a mind of its own. Each must be taken down.' Trudy probably echoed many people's feelings by remarking that she didn't like change. William replied: 'That which does not move becomes an epitaph to the past that destroyed the future.... Structures have been a prison of the mind. The mind of man must stop passing the buck.'

Central to my message now is that the structures on which humanity places its mental and emotional reliance – religious, philosophical, economic and the rest – are beginning to fall apart. We are seeing the effects on our lives every day. This is an essential stage in our evolution. For our consciousness to expand and evolve, we must free the creative aspects of our minds by stepping outside the structures and doctrines which have been imposed on us for so long. Of course this appears threatening to those who rely on belief, doctrine and external structures for a sense of support. But ultimately to be free of them is an essential step on the road to spiritual self-empowerment. Of course, the transitional period means that there will be many people who will be afraid; helping those people is central to the work of the Source. Throughout the planet Centres of Light are needed to heal the results of this change and help individuals find their own power.

Later, we were told:

There is much also to be said on the planetary mind, on the evolution of mind and evolution of the planet. There is to be a gigantic shift in the way the human energy exists on this planet and that is to be achieved in a relatively short period of your time. The evolution of consciousness which follows it will bring an end to the physical interactions of human resonances which are at so much dispute and destruction.

All the structures have to be looked at, for people will ask questions. The nature of matter and mind, of the structures of etheric bodies, astral bodies must be looked into deeper and explained according to Source Energy and brought into a realisation of the true nature of consciousness.

This will take time; you must be patient. It will be done, and it will be made into a pattern like a jigsaw which can be fitted together. There will always be puzzles, there will always be questions and, in the human resonance, there will be fears and doubts because one of the central messages of this work is that some of the structures which people have thought of as objective, omnipotent and overseeing are not in that form at all. There will be much objection. If you take away the crutches of a cripple, you must restore his legs otherwise he will fall over, and the idea of this is not just to take away the crutch but to give new limbs.

It is not a question of destruction. There is going to be destruction of structures not because you are doing it on your own but because structures have become the prison of the human consciousness.

The people who stay with you are those that are willing and will find a way to see that, when you are halfway up the mountain, you are in fact totally safe because the mountain itself is part of the observance you have. Its size, its overwhelming stature is part of that consciousness that you have learnt to observe, and when you see what it really is – that is, an energy with a probability factor that does not stay set – you can walk through the mountain.

At a later meeting we received more channelling on the nature of consciousness.

> Consciousness within the Vortex of human ideas has been standing on the rim of a wheel, from where it can only look out. Consider the change in consciousness, the evolution of mind which will lead away from the Vortex, to be a turning of all heads until they see into the centre of the wheel. In the centre of the wheel is a point where all minds can come and the curvature of space-time and dimensional influence can take them beyond and out of the Vortex.
>
> This is the model for the new conscious evolution. No more looking out into the endless curvature of space-time, but looking in to where there is escape and freedom and one-ness.

One further manifestation of spiritual energy was yet to come. Throughout my life music and sound have, as you will have gathered, been very important to me. Now, in the Monday night circle, this facet of my gifts came to fruition. For this we had to wait until the New Year. On 27 January 1992 I was deep in trance, channelling, when my Voice announced:

> We are going to start giving this group a demonstration of materialising sound, which Geoff is going to use as part of his work. We are going to show it to you first.
>
> Sound has a particularly interesting vibration, for it can be one of the transitions between the energy we use and the physical energy. Also, because of its familiarity and because of its joining together with all the creative forces at once, it becomes a complete

energy on all levels. We have been experimenting with turning the energy that is not physical into sound which is distinctly physical.

As an experiment for the whole group we have decided that it would be useful to take the energy of each individual within the circle and to make it a coherent note for each of you. That is, a sound which reflects an aspect of the energy that you have, that is of Source Energy.

This particular experiment represents taking an energy which gives you a link with the Source that you can use for meditation. We are attempting to take an energy within each of you and to cause it to resonate in sound and produce a note.

We were told that we were to record the notes, which would come in a particular order, one for each person in the group.

What happened next was quite magical. As we sat quietly, the air of the darkened room was filled with a sequence of delicate chiming notes. Each person heard their own tone close to him or herself. When we shared our personal experiences of the sounds, Trudy commented that she was reminded of Shakespeare – 'Each planet, each star in its motion like an angel sings.' When she heard the notes, she said they sounded just like the stars. The channelled reply came:

Indeed, and it is accurate to say that when the Greeks spoke of the music of the spheres, they had an understanding. It has been misinterpreted, often by modern thinkers, that this is purely a philosophical concept. They had an understanding that sound is not purely a one-dimensional matter. It has a resonance that has consciousness within it,

and we are going to bring it into the work because
for many people it will be a way of opening a door
and will become an interesting therapy for them.

The experiment was repeated the following week, and
we were able to make a better recording. For each person
there came a rushing sound, something like white noise,
followed by a clear, bell-like tone with gentle modula-
tions. These sounds, we were told, were representative
notes of our energies.

After I came out of trance, my Voice explained to me
personally that sound would become very important in
my work; that I would start to use these tones as a way of
opening people's minds for healing on a spiritual level.

13

Healing

Sound has become very important in my life as a way
of working with people. Once this particular door had
been unlocked, I found that the best way to manifest it
was to use crystals as a focus. I will hold a crystal in my
hand and when the energy is resonating well it emits a
small, bell-like tone, the actual notes varying according
to circumstances. This physical manifestation of spiritual
sound can have a profound effect on both individuals and
groups.

By mid-1992 all the events of the past few years were
coming together for me – the setting up of the Monday
night group and the manifestation of oils, crystals and
sounds, together with the channelled philosophy about
our perception of the universe, the breaking down of
structures and the possibility of opening up human minds
to new dimensions.

I could now be open about my role: that I had come
from the Source in order to pass that energy on to others
in a material or manifested way, to empower them to

make their own connections with Infinite Mind. <u>To empower others</u>, I believe, <u>is the true role of the teacher.</u> My task is to let people know that there is a force available to show them how they can participate in spiritual evolution. My gifts are simply a means of demonstrating what is possible, and they are only valid in so far as they open up people's minds to their own potential. It is only through individual development that the Vortex will evolve, and return to a state of spiritual freedom.

In October 1992, this was confirmed to me through channelling:

> You are one of the few sent here at this time. You will be respected and reviled, loved and hated, but with the total knowledge of being with the Source you will be able to reach out without fear. Collectively, we are here now to open the doors of perception for the evolutionary changes which must come. The planet and the universe are external and internal, they cannot proceed separately. You are one of those who are here to reconnect people with their true spirituality, which releases the love that is the creative force of Infinite Mind, so that their vision expands and the energy of harmonic evolution is seen and used towards a wonderful future of transition.

Another year full of change, 1992 saw the break-up of the Monday night group and the development of the group with whom I now work. As well as working with sound, I did an increasing amount of private healing and public channelling. I also began to travel regularly, taking my message to other parts of Britain and other countries. It is clear from the response I get that people are very open and that there is a need for what I have to give them.

The Monday night group continued until March at our house in Ealing, and further important information was channelled to us. But the group itself began to come naturally to an end: clearly it had achieved its original purpose, and now it was time for new energies to come in. While the break-up of the original circle was sad in some ways, it was positive in others. Roger, Rosemary and Trudy had helped me to bring the start of my work into reality; now they were free to pursue their individual paths. All three have remained good friends with Karen and myself, and they tell me that the group changed not only their lives but also the lives of others who have crossed their paths.

If groups are to be creative, their make-up will naturally change over time. They are not meant to be fixed, and during the next stage others would be supporting me. Karen and I started another group on Monday nights, still at our home. Of the many people who had come to me over the years to develop their healing and spiritual potential, a very few – as I expected – also had latent Source Energy. The time had now come to bring them together to form the next Source group.

One member of the new group was Suet Wan Thow, a young Malaysian woman who specialises in Native American drumming, flute and voice work for healing. She has a gift for enabling people to reach inside themselves to find their creativity and true self-expression through sound and rhythm. We began giving workshops together, at which I demonstrated the manifestation of oils and my own way of working with sound, through chanting and crystal tones.

I use these tones in healing and, more importantly,

to connect people with Source Energy; actually hearing the sounds allows them to know that they are with the Energy. They can be recorded so that recipients can listen to them and chant them at home to help with their own healing. Different notes are given in relation to different parts of the body and the subtle energies. The notes do not always follow the Western scale, and include quarter-tones; they vary as people's energies change and become more harmonious. They have a distant quality about them, with a kind of echo even when the room has no acoustics. To me they are profound and spiritual notes which are offered to those who wish to receive them.

In a group, the healing process can be enhanced by having everyone chant a particular person's note or notes. This can produce very powerful and beautiful results, affecting those receiving them on an emotional and spiritual level, and helping them to break out of their conditioned patterning.

The crystal itself does not make the sound: it is simply the focus for the spiritual source that I bring through. Everything has its own energy, which can be altered; I have produced similar sounds from other objects like stones from the garden. At one residential weekend workshop the group experimented out of doors. We meditated under an oak tree and were all overwhelmed when four bell-like tones issued from the tree.

When I work with a group, I prefer to allow the energy of that group to be part of the sound I manifest; I can sense it building up until the tones are ready to be heard. This is occasionally difficult if the group is not very cohesive, and I need to be in peaceful, harmonious surroundings for this work. Now that I have a Centre to work from, I have decided to reserve the crystal sounds for those who come there, so that the atmosphere and conditions are always right.

This manifestation of tones extends the perception of sound in those who hear them beyond the normal physical boundaries, by bringing the subtle and spiritual energies into a physical realm. Some of these energies cannot be translated into the material world. Those I produce represent a resonance, a bridge between this reality and the many spiritual dimensions. So there is not only an audible sound which everyone experiences as physical reality, but listeners who can open up their minds and hearts can feel the spiritual energy which is both within and beyond the sound.

In this respect there is a similarity to channelling: anyone listening to information channelled from the Source should be aware that the spoken words are only a part of what is actually available. No words can adequately convey the reality of the profound energy to which they are connected. Listeners have a responsibility to hear not just with their ears, their intellect and their judgment, but with all their energy. Both words and sounds, resonating as they do with the dimension from which they originate, can help to open the receiver to the potential of that dimension.

It is all too easy for some people to regard the crystal sounds as an amazing phenomenon, without truly understanding what is being offered to them. But those who are ready have an inner feeling, and sometimes even an inner hearing of the power that accompanies the tones. If they are touched by it, they can sense their own connection with Infinite Mind, the spiritual aspect of their being. It is as if people are already wired up for that connection to be made: my task is to throw the switch.

This reconnection is a step in our journey out of the Vortex. Within each mind there is a memory, a resonance of our original link with Infinite Mind. Some people are more aware of it than others, but it is part of every human being's spiritual inheritance. The more people are reminded of and reconnected with Infinite Mind, the more they are enabled to grow towards it. This, for me, is the real purpose of healing; it is my own purpose and what I most want to do.

When I manifest sounds in this way each person will respond at their own level, and some people's responses make it all worthwhile. I remember a woman who came up for healing after a public talk; she didn't ask for anything, or tell me what was wrong with her. No words were necessary at all. I told her, 'You can tell me what you would like.'

She said, 'There isn't anything I have to ask, I just want to be connected.' When she had received her sound, she didn't speak, but she looked radiant. She got up and left, beaming.

Physical healing can also be effected through sound. In simple terms, sound at the physical level causes vibrations: therefore the body's molecules change when sound resonates with them. When that sound accompanies spiritual intent, it can produce changes for the better. I take the view that the Vortex is an intelligent system, and so everything within it has consciousness, including molecules. Therefore the movement of molecules through making or receiving sound brings about a movement of consciousness within the body. If that state of consciousness happens to be an illness, sound can on occasion bring about a change towards greater physical harmony.

We should also pay more attention to the environmental noise which we have come to accept as a fact of life, but which may actually have a negative effect on our energies. We need to be more aware, especially in our industrial society, how continually we are surrounded by noise pollution in the form of traffic, machinery and so on. On a personal level, this can be countered by taking five minutes in the day to sit quietly, being at peace and letting go of stress. On a social level we need to be more active about getting things changed – not by violent protest, but by being aware of the noise we both hear and make, and passing this awareness on to the next generation.

The energy that works through me exists in many different dimensions simultaneously. This is what enables me to do what I do. Because I am not restricted by or to this dimension, I can go into other dimensions and bring through gifts like crystals and oils, in a way that is often considered miraculous.

Another gift that creates quite an impression on people is the ability to bilocate – that is, to appear in two places at once. Fantastic though this may sound, there are other recorded cases of bilocation in the literature of paranormal and spiritual research; Sai Baba is one contemporary example.

At a seminar in Switzerland in 1992 I bilocated twice. The first time was during a public demonstration when I gave healing to a man with very bad thrombosis; his main symptom was severe pain when walking. I gave him healing, and then told him to go for a walk. I knew I would go with him, but at the same time would stay on the platform.

I told the man, 'You're going to be fine. Go for a walk, you'll be quite safe.' And I made a mental promise to look after him.

While I continued my demonstration on the platform, he went outside and took a walk of perhaps a hundred metres; when he returned to the hall he was delighted, having suffered no more than a slight twinge. He said:

'Not only do I feel better but I really thank you for coming on that walk with me.'

I had literally been in two places at once. My mental promise had been enough to give him my physical company.

On the second occasion I was in the hotel where the seminar was held, chatting with an American psychoanalyst, when she said, 'What were you doing wandering round the hotel lobby yesterday? I waved at you, and you didn't acknowledge me. It was definitely you – you were wearing the same clothes.'

At the time she had seen me I had in fact been at a friend's flat, where I had gone to bed early with a book and a cup of tea. I had no recollection of being in the hotel, and at the time the woman had seen me I had actually been asleep. I was obviously happy to be in the hotel, and the energy I had been using all day was enough to create a thought-form which was seen by someone who knew me.

I also have the capacity to disappear. Once in the Monday night group, in trance, my body density faded to the point where I became quite translucent, and the others could actually see through me. I was in a state of consciousness in which I was able to move out of my body, taking some of its density with me. I believe this was a glimpse of what the physical body will be like some day in the future; as it evolves, it will become less heavy.

I do not often bilocate my physical body as part of my work. It is much more common for me to manifest sound and oils, while crystals and aromatic ash appear both when I am healing and at other times. I can produce these at will and can materialise crystals in specifically requested colours if it seems appropriate. It is a way of giving someone more than a physical cure, by reaching out to their spiritual being.

For example, I was healing a woman who had a traditional view of the colours relating to the chakras. The seven chakras or energy centres aligned down the human body are said to reflect the colours of the rainbow, from violet at the crown to red at the base. My own view is that if you sense or see or desire a particular colour while opening your spiritual perception through healing or meditation, you can trust that it is right for the chakra in question. This woman visualised her heart centre as green, so for her I materialised a small green crystal. This consolidated her healing by giving her a direct link to her own inner healer.

Recently I asked another of my patients, a young woman who had come for channelling and healing, 'What colours do you like for healing?' She said, 'Blue,' which is fairly commonplace. I said I'd see what I could get for her. Then she suddenly added, 'I like white as well.' And a little crystal appeared, blue at one end and white at the other. This kind of gift totally changes people's perceptions.

This is not something I do on demand, although some people ask me to. Once a woman asked me for some gold. I wondered about her motivation, but said I would see what I could do. What materialised was a piece of pyrites, perhaps better known as 'Fool's Gold'.

Not all my patients receive manifestations in the form of oil, crystals or sounds, or not on every occasion. For me, whatever occurs during a healing session, the purpose is to reconnect people with their Infinite Selves.

A lot of the conflict we see within the Vortex arises because, at a subliminal level, everyone knows that they have a spiritual self which they can't quite reach. That tends to make them bitter and frustrated, and they take it out on others. My message is that <u>everybody can reach their own spirituality,</u> but not by accepting imposed doctrines which limit their spiritual potential, nor by exercising their power solely for themselves. Healing is the most powerful and caring and loving force that can help people to change, to make the reconnection with their true spiritual being.

In fact I prefer not to be labelled as a healer, since the word 'healing' is generally understood to mean being made better from a pain or illness. As I see it, physical recovery can be a side-effect of the change of consciousness that occurs when someone is touched for a moment by this Energy, and it is this which enables them to find the healing within themselves.

The actual transfer of energy is instantaneous. The healing process happens outside time, since the energy comes from a dimension beyond time. There have been examples in healing of quite severely ill, physically damaged people apparently undergoing miraculous change. This is because for some reason the people concerned have touched that part of Infinite Mind where instant change is possible. For the majority, however, healing will speed up recovery but will not be instant.

If a person's belief system expects a time factor – and that is true of most people – then recovery will take time; how long depends on what is best for that person, which mainly depends on their psychology. If your body is sick because a car ran you over, that is a fact. At the same time, a part of your psychology may be delaying recovery because basic conditioning teaches us that an injured body takes time to heal.

Sometimes, if I sense that the person is open to it, I may say, 'Let's just presume that there doesn't have to be a fixed time – let's presume it can happen more quickly,' and sometimes it does. Instantaneous healings happen when the person receiving the healing has a close enough connection with Infinite Mind to realise that their perception has altered. For instance, when I give healing after a public talk the people concerned are usually with me for a few minutes, yet some go through major changes – like the man who had been suffering with terrible depression, and came back the following week to tell me it had completely lifted.

But you can't always take away people's belief structure overnight, nor would it necessarily be good for them. Beliefs involve not only the conscious but also the unconscious mind. Whatever belief structure healing rests on, in the end healing, to me, takes place at a level of consciousness within the person being healed, when they understand: 'You do not have to see yourself as sick. Change that perception and your body will change.'

Healers today work in a variety of ways, and many of the processes they go through are based upon particular systems. If a healer believes that it must take time to rebalance the body's subtle energies, then that is valid for them and it is right for them to work in that way. I would not wish to devalue those healers who work from within the Vortex. It is true that without Source Energy they cannot take people into the level of transcended energy that a Source person can, and they cannot change matter so easily. But a number of healers today are aiming not to cure physical symptoms but rather to connect people with their Higher Selves. I see the Higher Self as a thought-form within the Vortex, but it is nevertheless a communication bridge between the individual and Infinite Mind.

For me the whole purpose of healing is to allow people to empower themselves, and to take responsibility for themselves. Self-responsibility is a popular concept in healing and New Age circles, but it can be misinterpreted as: 'It is your responsibility that you are ill or unhappy. You have created your illness.' I would never say to anyone, 'You are responsible for your illness.' A lot of people are suffering today because of the thought-form that it is their fault that they are ill. Feeling guilty does not improve the health. I believe that the light of healing will help people to discover their part in their illness if there is one, and to address it with kindness and love, not with self-blame. It is not for me to judge right or wrong, and at the level of Infinite Mind there is no judgment.

Very often when I give a public talk someone asks: 'As illness is always caused by doing something wrong, do you think it's fair to take away the symptoms by healing it?' It's a loaded question because it makes two assumptions: that illness is caused by doing something wrong, and that healing only removes symptoms.

The answer which is channelled through me ignores both assumptions. It is quite simply: 'The Source gives healing to people as a spiritual unconditional gift. It is an intelligent force and will therefore help at the level which is appropriate. This may include bringing to their consciousness a cause which they may address.'

Of course I welcome people who come to me for healing for purely physical reasons; I like to be able to help. But freedom from pain or illness has another side: every now and then someone who is healed by the Source will start wanting to know more. Even if they do not respond immediately in this way, when I give healing I am in a sense offering them an energy that will remain with them, even when they die and beyond.

As this energy reaches more and more individuals,

whether through healing or other means, it is gradually affecting the whole of humanity. Because we are all interconnected there is a resonance going on around the planet. People are being changed, even those who have not deliberately set out to receive healing.

Self-empowerment does not exclude the need to help each other, or indeed for healing to be given in all its various ways. But any help that is given must encourage the receiver to find their own strength and self-worth. Nor should healing rely upon any doctrine which negotiates help in return for belief in that doctrine.

Many people today are seeking some kind of spiritual path – more than are generally given credit for doing so. They may start by exploring the wide variety of available information – reading articles and books, listening to tapes and going to workshops. Of course, you can learn from others, and it can be good to spend time with a teacher who has knowledge. But the first and most important step is to start loving yourself. When you love and trust yourself, you do not allow anyone to offer you spiritual enlightenment in exchange for your submission.

I am often asked how people can best help themselves, particularly if they cannot get to me or someone like me. There is no blanket answer; for some people contact with a Source person is necessary, and they can usually find their way to the right person. Some have the capacity to find what they need in themselves.

What I suggest to everyone who comes to me is to make available five or ten minutes a day, totally undisturbed, to carry out a meditational exercise whose sole purpose is to experience and believe in their own self-love. I also suggest ways in which they can consciously reconnect themselves with the Earth; many people today put their energy into looking upward for spiritual experience, whereas if they spent more time in touch with the Earth they would actually have a higher spiritual awareness. (Although I normally design these exercises for individuals, on page 222 I am including one that readers can practise.)

I would encourage everyone to search for their own answers, to accept only what feels truthful to you. In spiritual development, there is too often a sense of competition. Most people, no matter how far advanced they seem to be, feel at times that they could or should be further along the path than they are. But where you are is relative to your point of view. Whatever your walk in life, whatever your beliefs, you have a spiritual centre, and you can find it within yourself. Finding it doesn't necessarily involve words or formulas, or a particular practice, but starts by knowing that it is actually there. In spiritual terms there are no levels of superiority, no exams to pass. We are where we are at the time.

Of course, there are also some people who think they know it all. Once, in meditation, I received a very simple but profound teaching: 'You can always tell somebody who is enlightened because they won't have to tell you.'

My own growth took a further leap in the autumn of 1992 when the Energy I channel finally decided to adopt a name, Tareth. This could not happen until I could personally acknowledge the blending of the two minds: the Source mind and my own. The name Tareth has been chosen because it encapsulates in the physical dimension a link with Source energies in other dimensions, and brings them to a level at which the Source can communicate with individuals.

In November, I channelled the Source publicly for the first time using this name:

I am Tareth. This is the first time the communication has been made individual. The reason for the change is to create an energy which will more easily link with those who hear me. It should be remembered that I am still the Source Energy that has been explained to you previously. My identity is important only in the moment that it is observed. The true link is with the Infinite Mind and its probabilites.

I and the body I speak through are one. If you speak to one, you speak to the other. Each mind in its particular dimension is the One Source implant, whose purpose is to bring a change of perception to as many as possible in order to bring a change of energy in this dimension which is a prerequisite to evolution.

I have chosen the name Tareth not because it in any way represents a person or particular identity. I speak as an individualised form of all the Source Energy that at your present time is implanted in all the dimensions in the Vortex. It is as if I am in many places at one time. And it is this multi-dimensional link which gives to those who have Source Energy the abilities which are used to help change the understanding of as many people as possible.

You should always remember that I have no power to coerce any mind, but only the power to show what is possible. I can change perception and therefore can heal, open doors, and show you what is available. Only you can step through: only you can stay if you wish to.

I am always at pains to make it clear that when I refer to Tareth as 'he' or 'him' this is simply for convenience, not because he is an individual or personality. What is important for those listening is that Tareth's words and energy are there to help them experience their own connection with Infinite Mind. Often this is not conveyed so much through words as in the silences. The words are important in the sense of trying to make people aware of what is happening; but if Tareth reaches out and two or three people feel touched in some way, that empowers them.

At the time when I was given the name, my new group of supporters was taking shape; that autumn the energy within the potential Source people began to be activated. As well as Suet Wan Thow and Kath Cristof, at this time they included Sarah Shackleton, Caroline Frost and Lindsey McCleod. More recently we have been joined by Michael Osborne.

The membership of the present group may well change over time, but we share a wonderful sense of exploration. Recently, I have had a kind of realisation that although most of my life I have had friends, I have kept them to some extent at an emotional distance, so that it doesn't matter if they go away. With my present group, it suddenly does matter. They feel like a family. The change is interesting; one of the hardest parts of writing this book has been that the early years seem to be about someone entirely different, someone who is not me any more.

It was with this particular group that one of the most dramatic events of my life took place, which was to lead to the founding of the Tareth Centre in Glastonbury. It began in the spring of 1993, when we met one evening to meditate and Tareth channelled information to us about Glastonbury. He began by telling us that there is a basis of truth in every myth, and the myth has ultimately to be separated from the reality. Glastonbury is of course a focus for the Arthurian legends, which are quite a distortion of what actually happened.

The man who is now referred to as Merlin – this was not his name – had Source Energy and Arthur, far from being his protégé, was one of those who sought to take his power. Merlin was a spiritual teacher, with a group of eight followers, who used esoteric knowledge to heal and help people to understand their spiritual nature. His power was protected and largely hidden from those who were running society, because they would have misused it. Arthur and his kind were despotic tyrants, ruling by the sword, and Merlin's role was to try to prevent them from abusing secular and occult power.

Tareth explained to us that there are hidden energy centres around the planet which have been deliberately sealed up by Source groups; they are now being opened to help us through the current changes. One of these was at a place near Glastonbury where the stored energy and knowledge of Merlin's mind had been buried in the earth, to be released back to the planet at a critical time such as the present. Sound was one of the tools that Merlin's group used for healing, protection and creating energy, and tones were used to seal the site until its time of release.

What happened next in the history of my own group I hope to write about in more detail in the near future. Tareth told us exactly where to find the site at which Merlin and his group had sealed up the energy. In March 1993 Karen, myself, the group members and two observers travelled to Glastonbury for the weekend. Following channelled instructions, we found the energy centre – it was not at Glastonbury Tor, as some people might expect, and was well hidden.

Brimming with excitement, we went there after dark; at the site we sat in a circle and meditated. As the

14

Towards the Future

You are in the time now where preparation is being made. More than that – you are involved in the process. Your perception is part of the progression. Your ability to widen your awareness is part of the healing process between you and the planet. . . .

Real expansion of mind, awareness, growth and evolution lie within you all. There are no Messiahs to save you, only those who can help you open the door of perception in your mind. Any doctrine which teaches you that salvation is found only in believing another's word, adopting another's structure, giving up your responsibility and your own personal growth, is based upon the misuse of power.

It is from within that the changes come. I do not bring something magical that changes things. What I hope to do is to stir a memory of the future within some people, for it is all there within you. Those who find that memory stirring, I hope to help. But

I do say to all who listen, always, that there are many ways to find that truth. I am not preaching an evangelical doctrine and asking everyone to believe it. I have one way; there are many others.

But you must listen with the empowerment of self-love and self-confidence: do not be led by anyone who wishes to take your power away from you, for that is not the way evolution works.

These words were spoken by Tareth at a talk in the autumn of 1992, when he began speaking publicly of the need for everyone to take part in the next stage of evolution.

Particularly since the Source gave the name Tareth, the nature of the message I am here to bring has become clarified. It is a message that not everyone will like or accept, but it is a message of hope. I am here to say that we have choices. We can choose to participate in the evolutionary path that must be taken, and we can choose to reconnect with Infinite Mind, as we move towards becoming the spiritual beings we really are.

Many people are expecting an enormous shift in human consciousness to take place very soon. It is beginning, but the whole process of evolution is not going to happen in an instant, with a flash of lightning or a thunderbolt from on high. What we are moving towards is a genetically different human being, with a different consciousness, without greed and aggression, fewer in numbers and able to live in harmony with the planet. This cannot happen overnight, and will in fact take place over many generations.

The process must begin now, because it is essential for the planet and the Vortex it inhabits to evolve. The Source is helping us. Many people are already changing their perceptions and attitudes, aided by a new energy that is affecting the consciousness of those who are open to it. Tareth continues:

> Many of you are already aware that a change is taking place in the planetary energy. This change is the beginning of an evolutionary stage which to the purely human observation is a vital step. Although I will have more to say on human evolution, it is important to put it into context for the whole Vortex. For this is an evolutionary stage which affects all of it.
>
> Many minds have been through the physical stage that you are now experiencing and have moved on to further evolution. Each of these stages is, of course, important: it is a vital part of the experience that is growth. But now the whole Vortex needs to evolve. Without an interconnected evolution, and a realisation of the oneness of Mind, further movement and therefore further evolution will not be possible.

As we near the end of the twentieth century, some people are expecting a kind of Doomsday while others believe the golden New Age is about to begin. People seem to be particularly fascinated by forecasts of disaster, and are listening to all kinds of predictions from psychics and spiritual teachers past and present. According to some, our evolution will be accompanied or prompted by doom and gloom, cataclysms and disasters. The result is that many people are living in a state of fear and powerlessness, which are the very antithesis of the self-empowerment that will carry us forward to the next stage.

It is not Tareth's task to say, 'I am right and the others are wrong,' but to point out that there are other probabilities. You can make up your own mind about what has value for you. My own view is that channelling that comes from the Source is different in quality from predictions made by minds within the Vortex. It is more and more important for people to listen to the message from the Source, rather than those from the psychic dimension of the Vortex, entangled as they are with people's fears and desire for power. As Tareth says:

> Many prophecies have been about a new age, a change of being. Often, because of the structures of doctrine, they have been interpreted as a Day of Judgment, a separating of those who are to be saved because they have believed and kept faith, and those who will be cast aside because of their failure to believe.
>
> Others have spoken of enlightenment, of escaping the Wheel of Rebirth. Much of the inspiration that has come through those with Source Energy has been manipulated into doctrine, which can give great power to those who use it.
>
> It must also be remembered that once prophecy is put into the material universe it undergoes evolution in the energy of that universe. Prophecy is now being released from its doctrinal chains so that its true force can be put into perspective.

Prophecy is intended to show us what the potentials are, not to predict an inevitable fate. But when prophecy is misinterpreted and symbolic images are read as realities, they can become fixed in human consciousness and misused by the powerful in order to manipulate others. Prophecy then loses its true nature, which is not to predict but to help people to become aware. That situation is now being reversed.

It is vital to realise that *the future is not fixed*, even though there may come a point at which we are so set on a particular path that a particular future becomes inevitable. That will be our choice. But there is no blueprint. Futures are selected from a whole gamut of probabilities. The act of prediction entails selecting one of those futures in such a way that it can become self-fulfilling, possibly ruling out other potentials. To forecast disasters as inevitable is irresponsible, since people's belief and fear can then contribute to bringing about those very disasters.

It is true that we are at a point of crisis. We do have a choice, but we must take it now, while alternative probabilities are still open to us. The reason why Source Energy is entering the planet more and more is that a state has been reached within the entire Vortex that necessitates a major change. We do not need to be particularly spiritual to see that the planet itself is in a critical state, suffering as it is from pollution, overpopulation, the depletion of natural resources and the effects of wars, while for the first time in the world's history it is possible for human beings to use weaponry that could destroy the Earth.

But there is no reason to believe that the situation will be resolved by further cataclysms and disasters, or by comets hitting us from outer space. There have been disasters throughout history, and they have not turned humanity into a more spiritual species. As we have lost touch with Infinite Mind, the system within the Vortex has become flawed and out of balance. The state of our planet is a direct result of our loss of connection, and it is only through a change of consciousness that we will move forward. As Tareth explains:

Evolution is essential not just for human consciousness but for all the dimensions in the Vortex.

It will be apparent that the balance of energy on the planet you inhabit does not have a harmony. This is because this self-observing consciousness has now become so heavily entwined with an energy of isolation. It means that even on the individual level, many minds have lost the connection with the planet upon which they live. There can be no true evolutionary change while this disharmony is maintained. I and those who have come to help change perceptions are trying to put an energy here that will help restore the balance.

I and all those others who are trying to bring this energy to this planet are working, as I have said many times before, to change the energy of perception within individuals. Every person that I can help, every person who changes their outlook, causes an energy change in the whole.

The imbalances on our planet are largely caused by our own behaviour. Evolution cannot take place while we are overpopulated and while we feel justified in killing each other through war. Most of the suffering in society is man-made, not a punishment from on high. Illnesses like Aids and other auto-immune diseases, the increase in cancer, asthma and so on are the direct result of our own polluting activities which cause changes in viruses. When we destroy rainforests, there are fewer animals, fewer medicinal plants and less oxygen for us all. We have to know that we are not separate from each other or from nature. It is a reconnection with that knowledge that will change our thinking. The relatively few people responsible for these troubles must begin to be outcasts.

In addition to the man-made crisis, there is a great deal of talk in New Age groups about the Earth Changes.

Astrological forecasts have been made that in the near future the planet will tilt on its axis, bringing about a polar shift, accompanied by the melting of the ice-caps, tidal waves, asteroids falling out of the sky and so on. It is the view of the Source that this is not going to happen.

These forecasts are like the perennial prophecies about the end of the world, when members of sects build themselves arks or go up mountains to preserve themselves in order to found a new, enlightened human race. There are groups who hold the rather naive belief that they will automatically be safe because they are following a particular spiritual path or leader – some of them fully expect to be swept up to another planet when Armageddon strikes! I personally would not accept a place on anybody's ark (I have been offered one), because I believe that my role is to reach out to people, and if that means that at some point I will be washed away by a flood I will accept the situation. It won't mean the end of me or the end of evolution – and it could be the ark that sinks.

If we look at our history over the last decade or so there have been some really devastating breakdowns in structures – major floods in America and an earthquake in southern India, for example. If these had happened at, say, the time of a particular configuration of planets, some people would have fitted them in with the astrological predictions. Events which do not coincide with predictions tend to be simply ignored by the forecasters of doom.

There are also predictions of a shift in the magnetic polarity of the Earth. Although this is a natural if infrequent phenomenon, many people believe it will be tied up with our spiritual evolution. All living beings change polarity from time to time, and the Earth is a living being – or living process if you prefer. Its polarity has changed before and will change again.

Magnetic shifts may have effects on the climate, and indeed may adversely affect some parts of the population. But they do not occur with that purpose in mind. They are part of the Earth's living, evolving nature. We are supposed to be evolving with it. It is as if that process has become jammed, and now is the time to release it. Wiping people out won't give us a new society: the nature of perception has to change, and that is already happening.

It is true that human activities have put our survival at risk; the unmitigated ravaging and pillaging of the Earth's resources have caused weaknesses in the very structure of the planet. Like all living organisms, the Earth has its strong and weak areas. If humanity constantly puts out negative thought energy some of those areas of weakness will at times react to that negativity, just as a person with a weak back will suffer backache under stress. So long as we continue to mistreat the planet, we ourselves are likely to suffer.

The world will continue to suffer from eruptions and floods. There are always some people who alter their thinking as a result of major disaster, but an evolutionary change of the whole being must come from within. Arguments for cataclysms as a solution to the world's problems seem to make no sense. Destroying half the world's population would achieve nothing if the survivors were no different from before.

The evolution of the Earth means that there will be changes, but they will not occur either as a punishment for human bad behaviour or as an inducement to behave ourselves. They will in the main be changes of consciousness, manifested in the change of human

consciousness with which the Earth is intimately connected. The Earth Changes currently being forecast are,
I believe, simply symbolic of a new relationship between
humanity and the planet.

Increasing our awareness of the planet and taking
more responsibility for it are all part of a growth within
the human mind, and therefore a part of evolution. And
evolution is not just about rainforests, or pollution, or the
ozone layer, but involves the whole balance of the planet
and human consciousness.

The more people can connect with Infinite Mind,
the more they will feel and know that the situation is
not hopeless, that there is a joy to be found in life.
We do not have to struggle for it by setting ourselves
in conflict with each other or with nature. We do not
have to seek personal fulfilment through greed, envy
and aggression. We can realise it by renewing our
connection with the Infinite Mind within us, and by
working towards the long-term future even if we do not
see the results in this lifetime. This involves co-operating
with all the changes that are occurring now, and there
are many.

As well as the state of the planet, we are currently having to deal with the breakdown of structures of which
Tareth has so often spoken. Many people today are
alarmed and worried by the lack of stability in economics,
religion, politics, national boundaries, gender roles – in
just about every man-made, power-based structure,
in fact. Fear of the loss of power and security is also
giving rise to a backlash in the forms, for example, of
racism, fundamentalism and all kinds of bigotry. It is
important to understand that this crumbling of structures
is not something to fear, but a necessary and natural part
of the process of change, and a result of our growing

reconnection with Infinite Mind. On this subject, Tareth tells us:

There is no doubt that this is a time of crisis in planetary history. It is also a time of conflict. The conflict and the crisis meet together at this point and each of them becomes magnified.

The energy of evolution is implanted, and it will push its way through the concrete of power structures which would rather hold it back. At a deep level, in the consciousness of the planet, it is known that evolution is coming. It is recorded in the cells and the very genetic structure of every being.

As the changes are released, so is the history of those structures released. It is inevitable that breakdown means the release of that power. In one half of your planet you have already witnessed the crumbling of structures of political and social control. You have seen great, powerful conglomerates breaking down into cells. And within each of those cells, there is fear: fear of the past, and fear of the future.

To many, the essence of that fear becomes an overwhelming need to preserve themselves. And out of that need and that fear can come hatred for anything that is different, hatred for those who are not of the same race, or colour, or belief, or whatever structure happens to be useful to hang their fear on.

Remember that all is thought-form, and once thought-form becomes physical reality it can only be physically broken down. This process is not yet complete. You will see in those areas that I speak of those who will come and take away freedoms again, those who will try to restore the structures, and this will inevitably lead to conflict, and in that conflict many will fall. Leaders will rise and go down, and the power struggle will not be over for some generations.

Over the next three and four generations you will see attempts to build political and social structures. You will see them rise and fall and rise and fall again. Individual nations will grow powerful and then crumble, sometimes at enormous speed relative to the history that you are used to.

Planetary change comes from the connection with Infinite Mind, and no system can impose it. The unrest comes from the underlying energy of evolutionary change. As the grip of man-made structures loosens and minds can no longer be held, so the structures that came from the need to have power will fail.

For many of you in your own lifetime, and over the next few generations, doctrines which have become part of structural establishment will begin to crumble, and with that all the energy of spirituality that has been kept imprisoned will be released.

So, while much that is going on now looks, and often is, painful and frightening, the ultimate effects of the apparent chaos will be creative. We cannot have a change of direction without a breakdown of structures, and structures that have become physical cannot disappear in a flash.

Most of us want to see instant results, but it is important to think long-term. One of the problems with life today is that people are sacrificing long-term investment, like the ecology of the planet, to short-term gains like the exploitation of the rainforests and the oceans. We, today, must plan long-term for our spiritual wealth. For, as Tareth tells us, it is not going to come quickly – although the change has already begun, not only spiritually but genetically.

At present, the most serious problem with the planet is that it is having to support far too many people. Even if the world were totally populated today by positive, creative people, the planet's resources could not support them. Within a single lifetime, to the concern of environmentalists and scientists, the world's population has more than doubled to 5.5 billion, with a forecast of at least 7.8 billion by the middle of the next century. In order to reach the stage at which we can evolve, we need a population of about one-third of the present size.

From the point of view of the Source, there is no question of this being brought about by disasters, disease or wars. In order to achieve harmony on the planet one essential change needs to be made, and Source Energy has begun to bring it about. Tareth tells us:

> One question that comes over and over again is how can this planet evolve in harmony, while trying to sustain millions of people who do not seem to be in harmony with the planet or each other. The answer is that over the next century the energy of evolution will change that balance until the population is such that harmony will be possible. It is only when a balance has been found that a quantum leap of evolution can and will take place. There is an energy available now that will enable future generations to become physically transformed. Some will incarnate on this planet, many will not.

Mind does not die, and it is not necessary for every mind to incarnate physically to play a role in evolution.

Those who are open to the energy of change, and therefore able to change their perceptions, will continue to reincarnate on this planet. That does not mean that they will be the superior members of a chosen race; they will remain here because they have a role to play. Those who do not will have a mind role to play in another dimension; they will still be taking part in evolution. Some will be more useful if they are not physically incarnated, but are in the experience of Infinite Mind.

In order to reduce the population naturally and harmlessly, an energy has already entered the planet which is having the effect of changing our fertility. This process will continue alongside other genetic changes to open the probability of balance and harmony. The change will be linked to other energies in the DNA which will make it impossible for genetic scientists to interfere without damaging the organism. Over the next two hundred years or so the birth rate will drop to the extent that the world population will be one third of its current number.

Source Energy has made it clear that there is now no other way to restore harmony to this planet. Only when a balance is reached, when we can live in harmony with the body of the planet, can the evolutionary leap take place into the New Age to which so many people are looking forward.

Amongst all the uncertainties and upheavals in society, many people are seeking a meaningful purpose in life. Surely an important one is to open and attune to the spiritual evolution and to play a creative part in bringing it about. As we begin the long journey towards that goal, it is possible for everyone to find enjoyment and fulfilment in this life; surely the best way to achieve it is to be reconnected with the Infinite Mind beyond the Vortex that allows you to know for sure that there is a future, a hope, that what is happening here is flawed but temporary, and that we can work towards moving it on.

One of my own roles in this will be to set up Centres of Light to help those who are afraid or those who need guidance, healing and help with their spiritual development. Other groups are setting up similar centres all over the planet. Fear of the future is engendering all kinds of problems, distress and illness. Reconnecting people with their infinite inner selves will help them to understand that, although much that is happening now is unpleasant, the outcome can be joyful.

The more each individual among you understands and perceives your own spiritual nature, the more energy you put into that knowledge, the more you can contribute towards a future that will be unimaginably joyful. To conclude with Tareth's own words:

The crisis in the planet has to be solved in order for movement, which is evolution, to take place. But that energy is here now. Every healing is a chance to reconnect to the Infinite Mind, and every connection means a change of perception. Every change of perception now is an empowerment for the future.

Every healing puts an energy of positiveness into the universe. And every act on that level contributes towards the future. May I reiterate, there will be no Messiahs to save the world. There never really were. You are each your own saviour.

The Centres of Light which I and others are trying to create are for the purpose of self-empowerment, self-realisation. Every Centre of Light is a beacon guiding and encouraging those who are ready to move forward with the changes. If you love yourself in a truly spiritual way, without arrogance, from that grows confidence in your ability which is one of the driving forces of spiritual evolution. When you experience the energy of connection to the Infinite Mind, you will be able to perceive your worth.

So there is no need for despair at the conflict and the crumbling. Do not hide in shelters and wait for cataclysms to come. Reach inside and open the door to the infinity within. And those of us who wish to help you will meet you there.

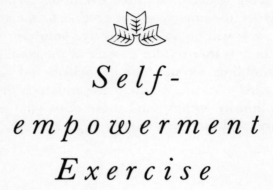

Self-
empowerment
Exercise

NOTE. *This exercise uses the name of Tareth in order to link you with the Source. I want to make it clear that this is in no way meant to be a form of prayer or worship. It will connect you with Source Energy, and make the exercise more powerful.*

The essential first step is a declaration that you are going to put aside time for this exercise. It is better to give a few minutes three times a week than to think now and again that you'll take half an hour to catch up. Be clear that this is your time and no one else's.

Then all you need is somewhere comfortable to sit in a room, the garden, or any place where you are happy to be.

Close your eyes. Then for one minute sit in silence. Notice any noises around you, but realise that within you there is a point of absolute silence that the noises outside cannot disturb. Allow yourself to sit quietly.

After a minute of quiet, start to notice your breathing. Breathing is an important part of the exercise, since it has a physically beneficial effect as well as helping your mind to focus. Start breathing very deeply, but gently, without forcing. Staying relaxed, allow your breath to expand into the bottom of your lungs. As you breathe out, let go of any tensions in the body. Don't worry about any thoughts you may have; don't try to stop them. Just let them come and go.

Now begin by linking to Source Energy by using the name Tareth, either as an inner thought or speaking it aloud if you wish. Breathe the name in on an in-breath, allowing the energy of the name to enter your body. Take six deep breaths, breathing in the name and relaxing as you breathe out. Then be still for around thirty seconds. Everyone's experience of this process is different. Do not stop to analyse, but continue the exercise.

Now that you are attuned to Source Energy, breathe in more deeply than you would normally. Imagine the breath going down your spine, as if the spine were a tube that could carry air right down to its base. As you breathe down to that level, you should say to yourself, 'I love myself.' As you breathe out, speak the words aloud if you wish. Say these words whatever they make you feel, no matter how difficult it is. On the next deep breath repeat them, and be proud and happy to say them – even if you don't believe it, be happy to say them.

On the next breath, say: 'I love myself as I am now.' This encourages you not to suppress or hide any of the thoughts you may have about yourself, whatever they are, but to accept that you can love yourself as you are now. If you want to change things, which you are entitled to do, it is important to accept them rather than hate them. This acceptance begins the process of change.

On the next breath, say: 'I am a spiritual being now and I am worthy of love.'

Repeat these statements, whatever they make you

think or feel. You may not believe the words – you may feel embarrassed, or sad. But whatever emotions come up, don't suppress them, and don't let them put you off saying the words.

Stop for a few seconds and again, on an in-breath, link to the name Tareth as an avenue to the Source.

Now sit with that energy for a while, allowing any thoughts to come and go, and be with the effects of the words you have just spoken.

After a minute or so, again focus on your breathing. This time, breathe even more deeply than before, imagining that your breath goes down your spine, right down your legs, through your feet and into the Earth (wherever you are). As you do this, try to sense and feel that the Earth is breathing as well.

As you breathe in, let the Earth's breath come gently into you, all the way in. Acknowledge the breath of the Earth as it enters you through the statements you have made about yourself and your worthiness.

Again, breathe into the Earth, even more deeply than before. Experience the sense of the Earth as a living being, with an energy circulation of its own. As you breathe in, imagine that you can sense and feel the circulation of its energy flowing through it, allowing it to come into your body. As you do so say mentally, 'I will allow my circulation to flow with the Earth's circulation. For a moment we will flow together.'

Relax and breathe again, even deeper into the heart of the Earth, imagining it as a real, beating heart. As you breathe in, think: 'My heart can beat together with the Earth's heart.' Allow the Earth's energy to flow into your body and mind. As much as you can, feel a sense of oneness with the healing power of the Earth.

On the next in-breath, breathe deep again into the

Earth and share your self-love with your love of the Earth. Draw the healing and the light from its centre.

Relax and be at peace with this knowledge. Don't suppress any thoughts, or try to force them away. Simply allow the breath and the heart of the Earth to be with you.

Breathe the name of Tareth again, and say or think: 'I am worthy to receive spiritual gifts, and worthy to move forward and evolve with the Earth, the spirit and the Source.'

Now sit in the quiet for as long as you can. Don't force this sitting; stop when you feel that you are losing your concentration or that you cannot do any more. Don't measure the time. There is as much value in two minutes of simply allowing this empowerment to happen as in three hours trying to make it happen.

You can do this exercise more often if you wish, but if you practise just three times a week you will be drawing on the amazing power of the Earth and the Source, which are coming together. You will find that your energy begins to change completely and you will start to realise how powerful, in a spiritual sense, you really are.

About the Author

Geoff Boltwood is an internationally acclaimed spiritual teacher and healer. He has been described as the 'English Sai Baba' due to his special gifts of manifestation and healing. He devotes his time to healing, working with others to promote increased spiritual awareness, and running his newly established centre, the Tareth Centre, in Glastonbury. Geoff also leads workshops throughout the UK and abroad and his work has been the subject of considerable media attention.

The Tareth Centre

For further information about the Centre of Light and Geoff Boltwood's work, send a stamped addressed envelope to the address below. Details of Geoff's channelling tapes are also available from this address.

The Tareth Centre
8A Market Place
Glastonbury
Somerset
BA6 9HW
Tel. 01458 833929

Piatkus Books

If you have enjoyed reading this book, you may be interested in other Mind, Body and Spirit titles published by Piatkus. These include:

The Afterlife: An investigation into the mysteries of life after death   Jenny Randles and Peter Hough

Ambika's Guide To Healing And Wholeness: The energetic path to the chakras and colour   Ambika Wauters

As I See It: A psychic's guide to developing your sensing and healing abilities   Betty F. Balcombe

Awakening To Change: Your guide to personal empowerment in the new millennium   Soozi Holbeche

Care Of The Soul: How to add depth and meaning to your everyday life   Thomas Moore

Colour Your Life: Discover your true personality through colour   Howard and Dorothy Sun

Creating Abundance: How to bring wealth and fulfilment into your life   Andrew Ferguson

The Energy Connection: Simple answers to life's important questions   Betty F Balcombe

Karma And Reincarnation: The key to spiritual evolution and enlightenment   Dr Hiroshi Motoyama

Living Magically: A new vision of reality   Gill Edwards

Many Lives, Many Masters: The true story of a prominent psychiatrist, his young patient and the past-life therapy that changed both their lives   Dr Brian L. Weiss

The Message Of Love: A channelled guide to our future   Ruth White with Gildas

Mind Power: Use positive thinking to change your life   Christian H. Godefroy with D. R. Steevens

Past Lives, Present Dreams: How to use reincarnation for personal growth   Denise Linn

The Personal Growth Handbook: A guide to groups, movements and healing treatments   Liz Hodgkinson

A Pocketful Of Dreams   Denise Linn

The Power Of Gems And Crystals: How they can transform your life   Soozi Holbeche

The Power Of Your Dreams   Soozi Holbeche

The Psychic Explorer   Jonathan Cainer and Carl Rider

Psycho-Regression: A system for healing and personal growth   Dr Francesca Rossetti

Reincarnation   Liz Hodgkinson

Rituals For Everyday Living: Special ways to mark important events in your life   Lorna St. Aubyn

The Secret World Of Your Dreams   Julia and Derek Parker

Spiritual Healing: Everything you want to know   Liz Hodgkinson

**Stepping Into The Magic: A new approach to
 everyday living**   Gill Edwards
**Teach Yourself To Meditate: Over 20 exercises for
 peace, health and clarity of mind**   Eric Harrison
The Three Minute Meditator   David Harp with Nina
 Feldman
**A Time For Healing: The journey to
 wholeness**   Eddie and Debbie Shapiro
**Transformed By The Light: The powerful effect of
 near-death experiences on people's lives**   Dr
 Melvin Morse with Paul Perry
**Transform Your Life: A step-by-step
 programme**   Diana Cooper
Working With Your Chakras   Ruth White
**Yesterday's Children: The extraordinary search for
 my past-life family**   Jenny Cockell
**Your Healing Power: A comprehensive guide to
 channelling your healing energies**   Jack Angelo
Your Psychic Power   Carl Rider

For a free brochure with further information on our full
range of titles, please write to:

> Piatkus Books
> Freepost 7 (WD 4505)
> London W1E 4EZ

PIATKUS

p. 61 - Chap. Shelley + definition
139 - William - intelligence
203-6 - Glastonbury